INSTRUCTOR'S MANUAL TO ACCOMPANY

THINKING THINGS THROUGH

Critical Thinking for Decisions You Can Live With

Dianne Romain

Sonoma State University

Mayfield Publishing Company
Mountain View, California
London • Toronto

International Standard Book Number: 1-55934-176-9

Manufactured in the United States of America

10 9 8 7 6 5 4 3 2 1

Mayfield Publishing Company
1280 Villa Street
Mountain View, California 94041

CONTENTS

INTRODUCTION

This text is designed to support interactive teaching. To use a motto that's been floating around my university, it's designed for the guide by the side, not the sage on the stage. I think of teaching as creating a class *with* my students instead of creating a class *for* my students. In the spirit of creating a class with my students, I invite students to select readings from the text and to recommend other topics and readings of concern to them. In my classes, students also participate in creating the class by making short presentations on critical thinking concepts and how to apply them. In addition, they teach each other by working in groups to do exercises, write papers, and plan their final group presentation.

To support interactive teaching, each chapter begins with a "Your Thoughts About . . ." section to give students and you a chance to find out where they are before reading the chapter. You need not always spend a lot of time on the essay at the beginning of each chapter, but you should spend some time checking with the students to learn what they think about the subject before launching into the chapter material.

The "Your Turn" sections within the chapters give students a chance to check their understanding of concepts in the chapters and to add their own ideas to those in the text. Students should be encouraged to do all the "Your Turns" that have answers in the back of the text. That way they will come to class knowing whether they have the basic ideas of the chapters. You may also select some of the open-ended "Your Turns" for class discussion or for ungraded freewrites.

COMMON PROBLEMS FOR STUDENTS

I've been using the material in this text for some time and have come across some sticking points for students. I've identified some of the major problems for each chapter. If you are new to teaching critical thinking, I suggest you glance over these. You'll be better able to deal with the difficult points if you have some forewarning.

SAMPLE ANSWERS TO EXERCISES AND READING QUESTIONS

I've included sample answers to the exercises and reading questions for each chapter. Please note that I call these "sample" answers for a reason. There could well be other equally good answers to some of the questions. And, God forbid, some of the sample answers could contain mistakes! Please do not treat these answers as gospel.

COMMENTS ON WRITING IDEAS

I assign lots of writing in my critical thinking class because I believe students learn more about writing and thinking by working on these activities together than by working on them separately. I realize that teaching writing may be new to some of you and that you may not have figured out ways to read and respond to papers.

Don't worry. Even if you don't have time in your schedule for grading a single paper, you can still ask your students to write. You can have students do guided freewrites using the ideas as guides. These freewrites need not be graded. They can be used to help students discover what to say in class discussion. You might consider having students write for ten minutes at the beginning of class at least once a week while you're taking role, putting material on the board, or recovering from a meeting you ran from to get to class on time.

The last writing idea for each chapter is a good one for a freewrite. It asks students to compare their ideas with the ideas in the chapter. This exercise gives students the opportunity to co-teach the class by adding their ideas to yours and the ones in the text. It also helps students synthesize the material in the chapter—to see how it relates to their previously held ideas.

Also, many of the writing ideas I've included are not to be written in the standard essay format. Sometimes students are presented a series of questions that ask them to apply critical thinking concepts to new material. These are no more difficult to grade than answers to short essay exam questions.

If you do plan to focus on teaching students to write, I suggest you don't overdo the number of graded writing assignments you give. I think college teachers tend to set students up for failure by giving them more writing assignments than any reasonable person has time to do well. Consider, for example, how many polished papers you could write in a four-month period, if you were spending much of that time attending classes, studying for quizzes, working to support yourself, doing your household chores, and socializing with family and friends.

I've settled on four short written assignments a semester (in addition to a short presentation on a critical thinking concept, two quizzes, and a group oral presentation at the end of the semester). As a rule, I have students prepare a draft for exchange with another student, and I allow class time for them to give each other feedback. I then give students another week to turn in a rewritten draft to me for comments and a grade. I also always allow additional optional rewrites so that students have an opportunity to improve their writing and to increase their total points if they wish.

If you want to assign papers but are worried about the number of papers you have to grade, ask students to write at least one of their papers with another student. Much real-world writing is done with others, so students may as well get some practice with the benefits and drawbacks of team writing before they leave the ivory tower.

If you are new to teaching writing, I suggest you take at look at Peter Elbow's books *Writing Without Teachers* and *Writing with Power*. He has lots of ideas about types of feedback to give on writing.

CLASSROOM ACTIVITIES

I've prepared some sample classroom activities for each chapter. I give a short description of the activity and set forth a number of purposes the activity is designed to achieve. You'll probably want to develop some of your own classroom activities. For ideas about how to design classroom activities I recommend Thomas A. Angelo and K. Patricia Cross, *Classroom Assessment Techniques: A Handbook for College Teachers*, 2nd ed. (San Francisco: Jossey-Bass Publishers, 1993).

Here's a classroom activity that can be used with any chapter (and any class).

Student/Teacher Dialogue

Description: Give your students two to three minutes at the end of class to write out a point they found particularly important from the reading or class discussion and a question that still puzzles them. Collect the papers and write short responses, then return the papers to the students so they can use them again the next dialogue day. (They need not put their names on the paper. Just pass the stack around the room. They will be able to recognize their handwriting.)

Purpose: The student questions will help you know what to focus on in the next class period, and the points the students write down will give you a sense that someone's getting something from the class. Questioning also improves students' ability to monitor their learning.

QUIZ QUESTIONS AND ANSWERS

As a rule, when I give a quiz, I give the students a practice quiz first so we can see where they are with the material. If most of them are not ready for the quiz, we delay it and do more practice first. The practice quiz gives me a chance to find difficulties that might arise from question wording and to gauge how much time the quiz will take. Also, by taking a practice quiz, students become familiar with the formal aspects of the quiz, and they can then focus their attention on the content of the questions.

Giving practice quizzes means, of course, that you'll need plenty of quiz items. I've listed a number of possible ones for each chapter. To supplement these, use exercise questions you didn't assign for homework. You'll also probably want to add questions that come from issues that class members have brought in for discussion and analysis.

In my class, I use only short, objective questions on quizzes. I evaluate more open-ended thinking and writing skills with papers and take-home assignments.

ACKNOWLEDGMENTS

I am grateful to Pamela Rosada for preparing a draft of sample answers to exercises and reading questions that I worked from in developing the answers here. Julie Thompson also prepared answers to reading questions.

CHAPTER 1
QUESTIONING EMOTIONS

This chapter teaches students how to become aware of, analyze, question, and modify emotional responses so they can use their emotions as guides to actions they can live with.

SUMMARY

Emotion is typically triggered by perceptions (what we hear, see, touch, taste, and smell) and consists of thought (interpretations, judgments, associations to the past, imagistic thinking), feeling (internal bodily sensations such as butterflies in stomach and pounding heart), and motivation to act (wanting to laugh, scream, flee, fight, reward, punish).

We develop emotional awareness by becoming aware of these various aspects of our emotions. Some people find thoughts more accessible. Others find feelings more accessible. Practicing guided freewrites helps us become more fully aware of our emotions.

We question our emotions when we suspect that our perceptions are partial and misleading. We frequently question our emotions when we suspect we have been given slanted information, from someone in a dispute, for example. We also question our emotions when we are uncomfortable with one or more aspects of them. We may not want to be motivated in the direction our emotion is pushing us. We may find the feelings of the emotion uncomfortable or the thoughts distracting.

We can change our emotions by changing what we perceive, by changing what we think including our interpretations, judgments, and voices from the past, by changing the intensity of our feelings, and by changing our motivations to act.

Some common constraints on our choices include adopting emotions to serve those who have power over us. We also unreflectively deny and reinterpret our experiences. We use unreflective psychological strategies to avoid anger and fear and also to produce and maintain positive and negative self-images. We can enhance our choice by becoming aware of these strategies.

Below are some common thinking mistakes that lead to negative emotions:

- *Catastrophizing:* Telling yourself that some things are awful or terrible when in fact they may be only inconvenient.

- *Misreading others:* With insufficient evidence, jumping to a conclusion about what another person thinks.

- *All-or-nothing thinking:* Applying a positive label to a narrow range of things and extremely negative labels to everything else (an "A" is good; "B," "C," "D," and "F" are all failures).

- *Hasty generalization:* Jumping to a conclusion that something will always happen, based on the evidence that it happened once or twice.

- *False fault finding:* Jumping to a conclusion that you or someone else caused something to happen when in fact you were only a partial cause or not responsible at all.

We can fill in these gaps and modify our negative emotions by focusing on the positive, seeking and accepting positive feedback, and suspending judgment.

We can practice similar steps for changing unsupported positive beliefs. By actively seeking positive *and* negative information and by being willing to suspend judgment when we have no solid support, we can cure ourselves of jumping to unsupported negative or positive conclusions.

Sometimes we realize we have jumped to a conclusion only after we have acted. By reflecting on our thinking, we can alter our emotion and decide on a new course of action. We can't always modify our negative emotions on our own. Some of our emotions are best examined in a therapeutic setting.

COMMON PROBLEMS FOR STUDENTS

When working on exercises in this chapter and throughout the text, students typically have difficulty understanding how the words are used. For example, in this chapter, the word "feeling" is used to refer to bodily sensations of emotion, such as pounding heart or dropping stomach. However, in everyday life, "feeling" is often used as a synonym for emotion. Thus, when you ask a student to describe her feelings, she will say such things as "I felt sad" or "I felt angry" instead of describing the bodily sensations she was experiencing.

Students also have difficulty understanding what is meant in this chapter by "perception." They sometimes take "perception" to mean intuition, insight, or evaluation. You'll need to emphasize that perception in the context of this chapter means what we see, hear, taste, touch, and smell. Also, I suggest you emphasize the difference between sensory perception and sensory imagination. When we read vivid writing—such as Danny Martin's story "Requiem for Mr. Squirrel"—our imaginations typically produce vivid sensory images, but we aren't in fact perceiving anything but the words on a page.

Finally, students have different emotional responses to what they read and hear and different levels of awareness of their responses. Some students have difficulty noticing that they feel anything at all. Other students have difficulty noticing their thoughts.

I have been pleasantly surprised to find that students are not uncomfortable writing and talking about their emotional responses to readings and exercises in this chapter. They seem to enjoy doing so. They particularly enjoy discussing their emotional responses with each other. However, I still recommend caution when discussing emotions. Be careful what you ask students to respond to and what you ask them to disclose about their emotional responses. Being asked to talk and write about emotional responses can be seen as an invasion of privacy, especially by students with histories of abuse.

SAMPLE ANSWERS TO EXERCISES

1. There are no set "right" answers to this question. Sensory images, judgments, and so on will probably vary from student to student. However, students should show that they understand the vocabulary of the chapter. They should not offer as an internal sensation something that belongs under the category of "judgment." Here are some sample answers for the ads.

    d. One might have several different emotional responses to this. Frustration with not being able to read Chinese would be one of them, or surprise and pleasure that something is written in one's mother tongue, if that tongue is Chinese. I experience some sadness when looking at the images in the ad.

       Sensory images: The ad shows a picture of a scale with a child on one side and a cigarette on the other. In the bottom right-hand corner of the ad is a cigarette being put out.

       Judgments: Cigarette smoking is portrayed as potentially harmful to children and as not as important as children. I agree with these judgments.

       Other thoughts: I also think about how difficult it is to stop smoking.

       Internal sensations: I have a bit of a letdown feeling of sadness when I think of children being harmed by smoke and of what people go through who try to stop smoking.

       Motivations: I am moved to continue talking with others about the effects of smoking and giving support to people who wish to stop.

e. I have mixed emotions. On the one hand I feel sorry for the child. Here's a breakdown of that response.

Sensory images: I see a little girl with big brown eyes. She's got her fingers in her mouth.

Interpretation: The girl looks vulnerable.

Judgment: This ad leads me to suspect that this girl and others like her should be helped.

Internal sensations: I feel my body droop a little when I think of children in Guatemala who need help.

Motivations: I'd like to help her and other children like her.

On the other hand, the appeal to a potential giver's self-aggrandizing wish to be a hero annoys me.

Sensory images: I see the language in bold type: "In her eyes, you could be a hero."

Judgment: People should be willing to help others without being called heroes. Ads shouldn't encourage such thinking.

Internal sensation: A sense of irritation.

Motivations: I'm moved to disassociate myself from a company that makes appeals of this type.

f. Once again, one could have mixed emotions when looking at this ad. It appeals to fear but could also annoy someone who recognizes the appeal. A person might also feel sorry for the man in deep water.

Sensory images: I see a man standing in flood water up to his waist. He's got his hand to his face in a gesture of worry or grief. Under the picture in bold is the sentence, "I never thought it could happen to me."

Judgments: This man's situation is bad, and it would be a bad thing for me to get into the same mess, but I don't think I will because I live at the top of a hill.

Internal sensations: I experience a quiet, down feeling of sadness when I look at this man.

Motivations: I don't feel motivated to do anything because I'm not worried about flooding, and there's no information about how to help this particular man.

2. There are also no right answers to this question. Student responses will vary.

3. Once again, there are no right answers. Whether students find something to question about their emotions depends on how they've responded in the first place. Here are some possible responses.

   a. Readers who want to work with severely disabled people but find themselves repulsed by the description of the boy with the enormous head may want to try to modify their emotional response.

   b. Readers may wonder whether Elena Albert's judgment of herself as "spoiled and quick-tempered" fits the facts of her childhood experience.

   c. Readers who love sushi may wonder whether they're going to deny the information contained in this piece.

   d. Readers may wonder if this ad gives sufficient information about the effects of secondhand smoke.

   e. Readers may wonder if this ad provides information about the best way to help this child and others like her.

   f. Readers may wonder whether people are as vulnerable to floods as this ad suggests and whether the National Flood Insurance Program (NFIP) is the best way to protect themselves.

4. a. Reinterpreting the outcome

   b. Blaming the victim

   c. Denial

   d. Denial

   e. Reinterpreting the outcome

5.–6. a. *Conclusion:* My confusion is all my own fault. Sally may not be solely responsible for her confusion. Maybe her teacher does not give clear explanations.

   b. *Conclusion:* I haven't done my homework. Leaving out one question is a far cry from not doing the homework.

   c. *Conclusion:* Maria was annoyed with me. Sabina jumps to a conclusion about what Maria thinks from how Maria sounds. Maria could have been annoyed for other reasons, and she may not have been annoyed at all. Maybe she was anxious.

   d. Forgetting to put out the material for recycling last night is a disaster.

e. *Conclusion:* None of the other tutors will be helpful. Li's jumping to a generalization from one instance. Perhaps one of the other tutors has more experience than the one Li first consulted.

f. *Conclusion:* I'll do really well on the rest of my homework assignments without working very hard. Jasmine's jumping to a generalization from one instance. Some of the other homework assignments may be more difficult for Jasmine to do.

g. *Conclusion:* They must not have minded that Jim talked nonstop for twenty minutes. Jim is not taking into account that the people he asked may possibly have felt embarrassed about criticizing him for monopolizing the conversation.

7. a. False fault finding
   b. All-or-nothing thinking
   c. Misreading others
   d. Catastrophizing
   e. Hasty generalization
   f. Hasty generalization
   g. Misreading others

SAMPLE ANSWERS TO READINGS FOR ANALYSIS

Danny Martin, "Requiem for Mr. Squirrel"

1. No right answer

2. No right answer

3. There are no right answers here either, but students should be using the terminology as it is used in the text. What they see are the words on the page. These words may trigger sensory images in the students' minds. Also, students should try to describe their internal sensations (heavy heart) rather than labeling them with emotion labels such as feelings of sadness.

4. No right answer

5. Whether a student's evaluation will change depends on how the student initially evaluated the warden. Students who jump to the conclusion initially that the warden had no reason to kill the squirrels and only did so to pain the prisoners may modify their evaluation of the warden after hearing the warden's point of view.

6. No right answer

Jonathan Kozol, "Ordinary People"

1. No right answer

2. No right answer

3. There are no right answers here either, but students should be using the terminology as it is used in the text. What the students see are the words on the page. These words may trigger sensory images in their minds. Also, students should try to describe their internal sensations (heavy heart) rather than labeling them with emotion labels such as feelings of sadness.

4. No right answer

5. No one right answer, but the answer should make sense; that is, a reader should be able to understand how the new information would affect the emotional response.

6. No right answer

COMMENTS ON WRITING IDEAS

The papers students write are to describe their emotional responses using the terminology of the chapter. They give students an opportunity to show their understanding of the chapter language.

Idea 4 can be modified to ask students to compare their emotional responses to one of the readings with those of at least one other student. The paper then becomes a comparison and contrast paper, and students practice their listening and recording skills in writing this paper. You can further modify item 4 by asking students to write this paper with another student.

The papers can be graded for the degree to which the student illustrates the basic aspects of emotion described in the chapter. They can also be graded on creativity, clarity of writing, and organization.

When making this first writing assignment, I talk with students about the basics of writing a paper, capturing audience attention and letting the audience know where you're going in the first paragraph, developing related points in the body of the paper, and finishing with the paper's basic insight and remaining puzzles or questions at the end.

For this particular paper, the content is pretty much determined by the assignment, but students often need help with how to attract audience attention, how to organize their points, and how to write them clearly. I talk with students about how to capture audience attention by starting with something puzzling, unexpected, or emotionally powerful. We analyze the readings for examples of strong writing. When I return student papers, I read passages from them that exemplify strong introductions, well-developed points, and effective conclusions to give the class more examples to guide them when doing their rewrites.

CLASSROOM ACTIVITIES

Questioning Common Assumptions

Description: Read these statements to your class before they've read the chapter and then again after they've read and discussed the chapter in class. Have the students jot down their responses both times for class discussion. The second time have them compare their before and after answers.

a. Emotion is very different from thought. (sometimes, always, never, no opinion)

b. Emotion and thinking are interrelated. (sometimes, always, never, no opinion)

c. When I'm happy, angry, sad, or fearful, I am aware of my emotion. (sometimes, always, never, no opinion)

d. I am comfortable with the emotions I have. (sometimes, always, never, no opinion)

e. When I have an emotion, I just have it. I have no choice about it one way or the other. (sometimes, always, never, no opinion)

f. When I am not comfortable with an emotion I have, I can change that emotion. (sometimes, always, never, no opinion)

g. When choosing what to do, I find it useful to follow my "gut" reaction. (sometimes, always, never, no opinion)

h. When choosing what to do, I believe it's important to put my emotions aside and look at the facts. (sometimes, always, never, no opinion)

Purpose: The first time you use these statements for class discussion you'll learn what assumptions your students make about emotions. You'll know what to focus on when going over the chapter material. The second time you read this list to your students, you'll learn whether your students have absorbed the basic points made in the chapter about emotion, thought, and action. Use disagreements you find with the chapter material as an opportunity to remind students of the points in the chapter and to invite them to give their reasons for disagreement.

To improve students' ability to monitor their learning

Comparing Exercise Answers

Description: Students form groups to compare and contrast answers to selected exercises (not more than three or four examples at a time or not more than they can do in ten to fifteen minutes). The teacher moves from group to group checking on students' progress and answering questions. The class reconvenes and reports back answers they've found, noting the statements that have "right" answers and the ones that do not.

Purpose: To develop analytic skills

To develop the ability to draw reasonable inferences from observations

To cultivate emotional health and well-being

To cultivate a sense of responsibility for one's own behavior

To develop the ability to work productively with others

Comparing Emotional Responses

Description: Students form groups of four and compare and contrast their emotional responses to one of the essays for analysis, using the concepts of perception, thought, feeling, and motivation. A group note taker writes down similarities and differences in their responses and reports back to the class.

Purpose: To learn concepts useful for understanding emotions

To apply these concepts to new situations

To develop the ability to distinguish between observation, inference, and evaluation

To develop the ability to work productively with others

To improve listening skills

To develop respect for others

Relaxation Exercise

Description: Turn the lights down or off. Ask students to sit in their chairs with both feet flat on the floor and their hands resting on their knees, palms up or palms down, whichever is more comfortable. They look forward and soften their gazes or close their eyes. You then lead them through one or more of the following:

* *Breathing.* Ask your students to become aware of their breath. Then ask them to take in a long slow breath, allowing their stomachs to relax to let the breath in as far as it can go. Ask them to hold the breath for a few seconds, then let it out again slowly, tightening the stomach and chest to squeeze out the last little bit of air. Repeat several times.

* *Visualization.* Ask your students to remember a time when they felt relaxed and comfortable. Ask them to imagine where they were and what was happening. If you are preparing them for a quiz or an oral presentation, ask them to remember a time when they took a quiz or spoke in front of others when they felt comfortable. Then guide them through the process of taking the quiz or giving the oral presentation you are preparing them for. Have them imagine receiving the quiz, reading through the questions, asking for clarification if they don't understand the wording of a question, and so on. Or have them imagine walking to the front of the classroom, arranging their visual or other media aids, turning to face the class, looking at the other students to see that they are ready to attend, taking in a breath, and beginning to talk, and so on. You can fill in the details that fit the test or speaking assignment you have designed for them.

* *Relaxing Muscles.* Ask your students to tighten the muscles in an area of the body when they take in a slow breath, then release the muscles when breathing out again. You can start with the toes and work your way up through the neck and face muscles. Or you can select certain areas to focus on, like the stomach, chest, and neck. I like to ask students to imagine scrunching up their brains, maybe scrunching their faces at the same time and then relaxing the brain and face when they exhale.

Expect some tittering from students who are not used to doing relaxation exercises. Let them know it's natural to laugh a bit, but redirect them to the exercise. Let them know that they may talk more about the exercise after it's finished. Don't be judgmental about their response, but also don't allow them to distract each other instead of doing the exercise.

Purpose: To cultivate emotional health and well-being

For additional relaxation exercises and information, see Luis R. Nieves, *Coping in College: Successful Strategies* (Princeton, NJ: Educational Testing Service, 1984) and Martha Davis, Elizabeth Robbins Eshelman, and Matthew McKay, *The Relaxation & Stress Reduction Workbook,* 4th ed. (Oakland, CA: New Harbinger Publications, 1995).

QUIZ ITEMS AND ANSWERS

Items

Here are some items to select from when preparing your quizzes.
1. True/False

a. _____ A change we make in a judgment about an event can change our emotional response to that event.

b. _____ Perception means judgment.

c. _____ In the text, "feeling" means the inner bodily sensation of emotion.

d. _____ Perceptions trigger emotions and emotions affect what we perceive.

e. _____ According to the text, moods and emotions are the same thing.

f. _____ We can modify the intensity of our emotions by taking deep, slow breaths.

g. _____ We can modify an emotion of fear by removing ourselves from a situation that triggers fear.

h. _____ We cannot modify emotion by changing our interpretations of events.

i. _____ Sometimes an association we have to a situation in the past affects the intensity of our emotional response to a present situation.

j. _____ Sometimes people modify their emotions to suit their employers.

2. Identify the following as examples of denial, blaming the victim, or reinterpreting the outcome.

   a. Joyce's co-worker says Joyce should have worn different clothes so her boss wouldn't have asked her out.

   b. Josh's friends say he should have moved, then he wouldn't have gotten shot.

   c. Josh's friends say they've learned an important lesson from Josh's getting shot.

   d. Josh stops reading the newspaper because he doesn't want to hear of the violence in his neighborhood.

   e. Sarah stopped doing breast exams when she found a small lump in her breast.

   f. Sarah's relieved to learn she has breast cancer because now she won't have to live with her suspicions any longer.

   g. If Sarah had worked on developing a more positive self-image, she wouldn't have developed breast cancer.

3. In each of the examples below, one statement gives evidence and the other states an interpretation or conclusion. Identify the conclusion and discuss whether you find the interpretation or conclusion questionable. Consider, for example, whether there could be other evidence the person is overlooking.

   a. "We all started talking about our weekends during the group discussions and didn't finish the task the teacher assigned in time to report back," Shelly thinks. "I won't work with those people again. It's their fault we didn't get done on time."

   b. "The first person I asked to be my lab partner refused," Juan thought. "None of the other students will want to be my partner, either."

   c. "My math teacher frowned when I walked by him in the hall," Kim thought. "I must not have done well on my test."

   d. "The explosion was all my fault," Lu thought. "I never should have agreed to be 'Wild Man Dave's' lab partner. I knew he would pull a stunt like this."

   e. "The teacher said 'excellent' to some students but only said 'good job' after my oral presentation," Jane thought. "I must have done a really poor job."

   f. "Suzy ran out of class as soon as it was over," Mary thought. "She must not have wanted to study with me after all."

g. "I just found out I've got a quiz in my biology class next week, and I wanted to skip class that day to visit with a friend from out of town," Joaquin thinks. "That's a disaster."

4. Do any of the following labels fit the thinking in the examples under 3 above: catastrophizing, hasty generalization, all-or-nothing thinking, misreading others, false fault finding? (If two labels seem equally fitting, explain why.)

5. Short answer

   a. How does the text distinguish between emotion and feeling?

   b. How does the text distinguish between emotion and mood?

   c. How does knowing your emotions help you to know yourself?

   d. How does Arlie Hochschild define "emotional labor?"

   e. According to psychologist Carol Tavris, what three psychological strategies do we use to maintain our belief that the world is just and safe?

   f. Define denial.

   g. Define hasty generalization.

   h. Define all-or-nothing thinking.

   i. Define misreading others.

   j. Define false fault finding.

   k. Define catastrophizing.

Answers

1. True/False
   a. True
   b. False
   c. True
   d. True
   e. False
   f. True
   g. True
   h. False
   i. True
   j. True

2. Identify

   a. Blaming the victim
   b. Blaming the victim
   c. Reinterpreting the outcome
   d. Denial
   e. Denial
   f. Reinterpreting the outcome
   g. Blaming the victim

3. Identify the Conclusion

   a. "It's their fault we didn't finish on time." Shelly fails to take any responsibility for the group's not finishing on time.

   b. "None of the other students will want to be my partner." Juan jumps to a generalization about all students from one refusal.

   c. "I did not do well on my test." Seeing her teacher's frown, Kim jumps to a conclusion that her teacher was thinking about Kim's test. Maybe the teacher had a headache, was on the way to boring meeting, or was worrying over not having read the tests yet.

   d. "The explosion was all my fault." Lu accepts full responsibility for the lab explosion but gives evidence to indicate that Wild Man Dave was really responsible.

   e. "I did a really poor job." Jane jumps to the conclusion that she did a poor job simply because she didn't get the highest praise.

   f. "Suzy did not want to study with me." Mary jumps to the conclusion that Suzy doesn't want to study with her because Suzy runs out of the class room. Maybe Suzy isn't feeling well.

   g. "That's a disaster." Joaquin jumps to the conclusion that something is a disaster when it is merely unfortunate. Maybe he can get permission to take the biology quiz another time, or maybe he can find another time to see his friend.

4. Label the Examples

   a. False fault finding
   b. Hasty generalization
   c. Misreading others
   d. False fault finding
   e. All-or-nothing thinking

    f. Misreading others
    g. Catastrophizing

5. Short Answer

    a. Emotion is a complex phenomenon typically occasioned by perceptions and made up of thinking, feeling, and motivation. Feeling is the internal sensation of emotion, such as a dropping stomach or pounding chest.

    b. Emotions tend to be intense and brief whereas moods tend to be less intense, less focused on particular thoughts, and more protracted.

    c. By knowing our emotions we know our values, and knowledge of values forms an important part of self-knowledge.

    d. According to Hochschild, emotional labor is inducing or suppressing "feeling in order to sustain the outward countenance that produces the proper state of mind in others."

    e. Denial, blaming the victim, and reinterpreting an event

    f. Denial is refusing to accept or take in information that would lead us to a conclusion we do not want to hold.

    g. Hasty generalization is jumping to a conclusion that something will always happen based on the observation that it's happened once or twice.

    h. All-or-nothing thinking is jumping to the conclusion that something went totally wrong just because it didn't go totally right.

    i. Misreading others is jumping to a conclusion about what someone thinks, based on insufficient evidence.

    j. False fault finding is jumping to a conclusion that someone is totally responsible for something when the evidence indicates at most that the person is partially responsible.

    k. Catastrophizing is telling yourself that some things are awful or terrible when in fact they may be only inconvenient.

CHAPTER 2
DECIDING HOW TO ACT

This chapter teaches students how to make thoughtful decisions by defining the problem, generating and choosing among alternative solutions, and taking preventive measures so the same problems don't keep recurring. It also introduces positive, productive ways to resolve conflicts.

SUMMARY

Thoughtful decision making is a process that helps us make decisions that we'll be less likely to regret. The steps include defining the problem, discovering alternative solutions, identifying the pros and cons of the solutions, weighing the alternatives, reviewing and deciding, and taking preventive measures.

Defining the problem includes gathering the facts, analyzing the situation, and setting goals. When gathering facts, you use your own background knowledge and experts' advice to determine which facts are relevant. When analyzing a situation, you are trying to determine causal relations. Sometimes you can do this yourself. Other times you need expert advice. When setting goals, you need to ask yourself whether some goals matter to you more than others, and you need to question whether the goals are authentically yours or whether you've absorbed them unaware.

Some techniques for discovering alternative solutions include research, role-play, brainstorm, and taking a break. Sometimes decision makers shortcut this step and use what's available. When the best solution does not occur among the available ones, decision makers commit the fallacy of accepting false alternatives or creating a false dilemma. The decision makers assume that they must take one of a given pool of alternatives when in fact there are other, better ones if they would search for them.

When identifying the pros and cons of a proposed solution, ask the following questions. Will the proposed solution meet the goal you've established? Will it have other, positive effects? Does it conflict with any personal or social values? What resources does the proposed solution use?

When answering these questions, people sometimes overlook the long-range effects of the proposed solution or the disadvantages of a preferred solution. Role-playing helps keep these in mind.

Sometimes decision makers shortcut evaluating the pros and cons of proposed solutions by asking someone to provide a nutshell briefing, a short report of the pros and cons of the various solutions. This shortcut can backfire when the one providing the briefing has a vested interest in a particular solution. In such a case, the briefer sometimes presents a weak version of a solution, then points out its weaknesses and recommends his or her alternative solution. This tactic is called "the straw person fallacy." The briefer knocks down a straw position instead of the real flesh-and-blood one.

When weighing alternatives, decision makers sometimes have difficulty because they encounter a moral dilemma: two or more of their deeply held values come into conflict. At other times, decision makers find that their values conflict with their immediate wants and impulses. In such cases, decision makers sometimes shortcut thinking through their values and choose from impulse. They act on the impulse to put themselves first, to retaliate, to avoid punishment, or to go along with the group.

Reviewing and deciding is made difficult because of uncertainty. It's important to remember that failure to make a decision also has effects. We can hedge our bets against uncertainty by implementing our decisions in stages and by preparing contingency plans.

Before making the final decision, you should review the decision-making process you went through to determine whether you took the steps you needed or whether you took shortcuts that may lead you into trouble.

Finally, it's a good idea to consider preventive measures to help you avoid the problem next time. You can use thoughtful decision making to decide which preventive measures to take.

When we make decisions with others, conflicts sometimes emerge. We can resolve these conflicts by listening carefully to each other, offering each other reasons, and brainstorming to find a win/win solution—one that meets the goals of everyone involved. We can also resolve differences by selecting a procedure such as flipping a coin, voting, or agreeing to disagree as a way to end a dispute.

COMMON PROBLEMS FOR STUDENTS

This chapter covers a lot of material in a short space, so problems can develop for students unless you select aspects of the chapter to focus on. Also, to understand certain parts of the chapter fully requires more information than is presented in the text. For example, to be able to analyze a situation, you often need a sophisticated understanding of causal reasoning or at least information about how to choose experts. Chapter 7 introduces questions to ask when selecting experts and Chapter 10 introduces the complexity of causal reasoning. Also, students will better understand the straw person fallacy after they've studied arguments and slanting in some detail. I introduce this fallacy again in Chapter 7.

I use this chapter to give students a gloss on the complexity of deciding how to act and to emphasize the importance of looking at a variety of points of view when making decisions. I also use it to motivate the study of the following chapters. I expect students to come back to this chapter again later in the semester when they are working on their semester projects, which require them to recommend a solution to a problem.

SAMPLE ANSWERS TO EXERCISES

1. a. Not really; we know he charged two other credit cards to the limit but we do not know why.

   b. Yes, Sally's housemates want her to watch TV instead of studying for her exam, which she needs to do.

   c. No. More information is needed regarding their relationship. Are they married or monogamous with one another, and sure of their HIV status? Are condoms their only method of birth control or could they use something else? Have they just met?

   d. Yes, one student monopolizes the conversation in one of Ari's classes.

   e. The problem is sorting through a controversy. The advertisement claims that the mass killings of the Holocaust didn't happen. Student editors who have published the ad claim that not publishing it would violate free speech. The editorial writer argues that newspapers are free to refuse to publish lies and that the claims in the ad have been proven to be lies.

2. a. Not enough information is given for us to know why Sam's already charged his other two credit cards to the limit.

   b. We can analyze it in that we know Sally needs to study. If she does not study, she will most likely do poorly on her exam.

   c. We can analyze the situation only by making certain assumptions regarding the relationship between the two participants. The problem was caused when they failed to replenish their supply of condoms. If nothing is done and they have unprotected sex, they run the risk of creating an unwanted pregnancy or transmitting a sexually transmitted disease.

   d. If nothing is done, chances are that the student will continue to monopolize the conversation. We have no information regarding what caused the problem; does anyone else want to talk?

   e. In this case, rather than thinking about the causes and effects of the controversy, it would be more useful to try to figure out the effects of publishing or not publishing the ad. Will not publishing the ad lead to the abolition of free speech, as one student editor claims? Is not publishing the ad a way of preventing the spread of known lies? This controversy is a problem for an editor who hasn't researched free speech issues and doesn't have background knowledge about the Holocaust.

3. There are no set answers to these questions, but students' answers should show that the students understand what a goal is, have thought about how their goals are influenced by others, and recognize ways their goals conflict.

4. There are many possible answers to these scenarios; an example is given for each.

   a. *Problem:* Class is boring.

      Opportunity: Discuss the problem with the teacher in an effort to improve class instruction.

   b. *Problem:* My apartment is too small for two people.

      Opportunity: Great! I'll get to move to a bigger place.

   c. *Problem:* If I do not accept the advances, I may get a poor grade.

      Opportunity: Educate the teacher about sexual harassment.

   d. *Problem:* Sara doesn't want to steal, but she doesn't want her friends to think she is a prude.

      Opportunity: Sara can talk to her friends about the morality of shoplifting.

   e. *Problem:* Paul is offended that his friends are only concerned about whether he had sex with his date, not how they got along.

      Opportunity: Paul can talk to his friends about his feelings.

5. The following alternatives are not intended to be all-inclusive of the options available, merely representative of the types of alternatives.

   a. You could go and not drink, you could not go and go out elsewhere . . .

   b. You could go and not spend money, you could not go and not lecture, you could go and return the sweater you bought last week that doesn't really fit . . .

   c. You could ask the teacher's permission not to dissect the frog, explaining your reasoning.

   d. You could try talking to the department chair who would, most likely, send you back to the instructor.

   e. There are numerous alternatives regarding welfare reform specific to teen mothers; only a few are offered here.

6. There are many possible right answers to this question.

7. There are no right answers to these questions, but students' answers should show that students understand the question. Here is a sample answer for (a): Disposable diapers save time (especially if you do not use a diaper service), but they fill up garbage dumps. Cloth diapers are easier on the environment, but they take more time and can be inconvenient. There may also be cost differences, depending on whether you use a diaper service. Generally, I'd put protecting the environment over saving time, but there may be times when convenience would matter more to me. I might use a diaper service as a rule but carry disposable diapers on trips.

8. There are no right answers to these questions, but the students' answers should show that students understand the question. Here are some sample answers.

   a. Me first, or going along with the group, instead of thinking about the long-range effects of your action on others

   b. Me first, instead of thinking of the needs of your family, or avoid punishment, if the family is threatening or "guilt tripping." (Maybe they have others they can ask for money. Maybe they have gotten themselves into this predicament by buying an expensive car. They could sell their own car rather than ask you not to buy one.)

   c. None of the labels clearly apply, as far as I can tell. But we could use a concept from Chapter 1: denial. I'd be inclined to want to ignore the possibility that I'd have to do something I didn't want to do in the army if I were really strapped for cash. We also need to be on the lookout for taking short-range effects more seriously than long-range ones.

   d. Avoid punishment

   e. None of the labels clearly apply, as far as I can tell.

SAMPLE ANSWERS TO READINGS FOR ANALYSIS

"Why I Am Not Going to Buy a Computer: Readers' Letters and Wendell Berry's Reply"

These answers will refer to Berry's original article as well as to the readers' letters and Berry's response to them.

1. a. Berry is concerned about the existence of strip-mining and the expense of computers. I would like to know more about the problem of strip-mining. I also think Berry could include the continual upgrading of computers.

   b. Berry draws a link between the use of computers and strip-mined coal. He doesn't explain the relationship explicitly, but computers run on electricity and strip-mined coal is used to produce electricity. James Rhoads claims that energy corporations are poorly managed. Perhaps he thinks that this leads to more strip-mining, but he doesn't say so. It would be useful to know more about the effects of the poor management.

   c. Berry wants to minimize connections with the energy corporations. He also wants to maintain his existing work relationship with his wife. At the end of his article he lists his standards for technological innovation, which imply these and other goals, such as to conserve energy, save money, and maintain small, privately owned businesses. A number of the other writers (Rhoads, Borenstein, Koosman) share Berry's concern about protecting the environment from giant corporations.

2. Berry chooses not to use a computer. He writes by hand, and his wife types and edits his work on a manual typewriter. Rhoads suggests that the energy corporations develop more efficient management. He also suggests protests against strip-mining. Koosman suggests that we support alternatives to coal-generated electricity and to IBM-style technocracy, but he doesn't mention any specific alternatives.

3. Borenstein points out the use of computers for environmental activism. None of the writers discuss the continuing upgrading and obsolescence that goes with the computer industry. They don't discuss what happens to the old machines when we get the new ones. They also don't discuss the degree to which computers save paper. A number of Berry's critics discuss the problem of generalizing Berry's solution. Many people don't have wives. Those who do may find that their wives prefer to do other work. Koosman points out that hiring a secretary would be much more expensive than owning a computer.

4. Inkeles mocks Berry and his wife's arrangement and Koosman points out the effects of making a general policy of using wives instead of computers. Berry has not suggested that everyone adopt his solution. These people credit him with making a broader claim than he has made. It's easier to knock the broader claim than to address the claim Berry actually makes.

5. I'd like to hear from Berry's wife. I'd also like to hear from the computer industry and from the electric companies. These are interested parties in this discussion whose points of view have not been expressed.

6. Yes, values come into conflict. For those who want to free themselves from energy consumption but still want to be connected with the rest of the world, the use of a computer poses a problem.

7. Yes, Berry's solution would not work for most of us. The other solutions were not spelled out fully enough for me to judge one way or another.

8. Berry mentions the intensity of feeling expressed in the letters. I'd like to discuss his explanation of this feeling. I'd also like to discuss Johnson's attack on Berry for being "impure," and Berry's response.

Juli Loesch Wiley, "Speech to a Woman Seeking an Abortion"

1. There are no set right answers to these questions; however, here are some points to consider.
   a. Woesch never actually addresses the issue at hand, which is to speak "about the operation," other than her remarks regarding emotional and physical trauma.
   b. No. She does ask the client to consider why she has chosen abortion, and she offers some options other than abortion, but she does not address the issue of the operation itself other than the survey results stating that 90% of women who have abortions experience physical and emotional trauma. She does not cover what the client can expect medically before, during, and after the procedure. (Note: there is no citation regarding survey source, and there is no qualifier supplied to define the severity of the trauma experienced.)
   c. She would prefer that the woman not abort the fetus.

2. There are no right answers to these questions.

3. She offers the options of adoption, raising the child yourself, and raising it with a spouse or family member for support. I don't know of other alternatives.

4. She mentions the physical and emotional trauma of abortion. She does not mention the emotional trauma of adoption or the financial and emotional difficulties of raising a child. Nor does she compare the relative health risks of abortion at different stages with those of childbirth. She raises questions that suggest ways in which abortion might conflict with deeply held values, but she doesn't raise any questions that suggest ways that adoption might conflict with deeply held values.

5. Yes, in almost every solution she focuses on only one aspect of the issue. For example, in number 3 she wonders whether it is "fair that you will be subjected to

physical, emotional, and spiritual trauma because they possibly have an anti-child attitude?" Perhaps they are not anti-child, but rather are realistic regarding their financial ability to rear a child.

6. I would want to talk to someone at a woman's clinic to get additional information.

7. There is no right answer here.

8. Answers would depend on the circumstances. Some women might have to watch out for going along with their peer groups. Others might have to watch out for fears of being punished by a parent or guardian.

9. Wiley doesn't specifically address this.

10. I'd like to discuss Wiley's language—for example, when she refers to the fetus as "your son or daughter."

Fredrick Turner, "Speech to a Woman Seeking an Abortion"

1. There are no right answers to these questions; however, points to consider are listed.

   a. Although there is no right answer to this question, it is important to note that Turner never discusses what a woman's options are should she decide to keep her baby.

   b. He does not cover what the client can expect medically before, during, and after the procedure.

   c. He is obviously pro-choice. In fact, the article reads as if he is trying to talk her into having an abortion. He explains that he will be giving her facts regarding abortion and that they will possibly discuss the morality behind the issue.

2. He does not discuss any of the client's options (other than abortion). Instead, he focuses on the issue of morality regarding abortion. He could have discussed adoption and raising the child.

3. Again, his discussion is about morality. He does not offer alternatives.

4. He doesn't consider other alternatives.

5. It would be useful to talk to others who know more about the medical effects of abortion. It would also be useful to talk with someone who has information about other alternatives.

6. Answers will vary.

7. He doesn't mention any. Some people don't have health coverage or money to pay for abortions or easy access to clinics that perform abortions.

8. I'd like to discuss the analogies that Turner draws or come back to this essay again when reading about analogical reasoning in Chapter 8.

Nancy Mitchell, "Options in the Face of Abuse"

1. There are no right answers to these questions; however, some points to consider may be listed.

   a. She points out that Anita Hill continued working with Clarence Thomas after the alleged abuse and that other harassed women do not report and do continue working for men who have harassed them. She says that Anita Hill was a credible witness and yet the majority of Americans didn't believe Anita Hill's story.

   b. She offers Hill's regard for Thomas and her concern about how he might help her career as explanations of why Hill continued working for Thomas after the harassment. And Mitchell notes that financial dependence keeps other women from speaking up about harassment. She claims that women can misevaluate a man's behavior because of his honorable reputation or because it "takes more self-confidence than many of us have to flatly reject attention from a man whom we have respected." She claims that Americans didn't believe Anita Hill because she waited so long to speak out.

   c. Mitchell doesn't explicitly express her goals, but I believe she'd like to see people believe women who are sexually harassed and that she'd like to see a decrease in the incidence of sexual harassment.

2. She suggests that women who are sexually harassed file complaints, tell friends and credible pillars of the community, document the abuse, and so on. She also says that women can try to make the best of the abuse. Finally, like Anita Hill, women can try to make the best of the abuse, then speak out. Her solutions put the full weight of the problem on the women who are abused. Other solutions to the problems of sexual harassment and of people not believing women who are sexually harassed would be for all citizens to have their consciousness raised, for more career opportunities to be available to women (to minimize the financial effects of speaking up or moving on), and for men to speak up about their colleagues who engage in sexual harassment.

3. Mitchell discusses the repercussions of delayed reporting (as Anita Hill did until it was "too late"): potential career advancement but lack of credibility. She also considers possible ramifications of early reporting: financial insecurity and humiliation, yet more credibility.

4. Not that I see

5. I'd like more information about the effects on women of early reporting. I'd also like to hear from women who have endured sexual harassment to save their jobs.

6. Some values that could potentially come into conflict would be career or financial security and integrity.

7. Certainly. I can imagine avoiding punishment or retaliating in response to unwanted sexual attention.

8. It might be difficult to implement her suggestion to tell others in an organization with no trained personnel to handle such problems.

9. A discussion of the meaning of sexual harassment would be useful.

Camille Paglia, "Rape and Modern Sex War"

1. There are no right answers to these questions; however, here are some points to consider.

   a. Paglia discusses date rape only at frat parties, and not in any of the other situations in which date rape can occur.

   b. She links college men's sexual behavior to their hormones and says that "hunt, pursuit, and capture" are biologically programmed into male sexuality. She does not discuss alcohol as a potential cause of a man's sexual aggression, but she does say a woman is a fool to get drunk at a fraternity party. She dismisses feminist claims that rape is an act of power rather than sex (though she says that men must struggle for identity against the overwhelming power of their mothers). She also dismisses feminist claims that we are affected by our environment. And yet she claims that "Generation after generation, men must be educated, refined and ethically persuaded away from their tendency toward anarchy and brutishness," which implies that environment can have some influence.

    c. Her main goal is to decrease the incidence of date rape. She also hopes to change the "feminist" view of date rape, educate women that they have the power and responsibility to decrease the incidence of date rape, and convince colleges to leave the prosecution of rape to the legal system.

2. Paglia discussed educating women about attending social functions in groups and acting responsibly when they were out. She also claims the only solution is self-awareness and self-control; this is an example of false alternatives. Because she doesn't see the connection between alcohol and date rape, Paglia doesn't suggest that everyone at fraternity parties drink less or not at all. She also doesn't consider the possibility of consciousness-raising courses for fraternities or of fraternities developing codes of ethics about sexual relations.

3. She does not discuss the pros and cons of her solution. For females to develop self-awareness and self-control is a great idea, but unless men develop these same abilities, the aware and self-controlled females may be ostracized and ridiculed.

4. Paglia stereotypes feminism with exaggerations such as "Academic feminism is lost in a fog of social constructionism. It believes we are totally the product of our environment." Many feminists aren't social constructionists to this degree. Even Paglia calls herself a feminist and apparently doesn't hold this position.

5. It would be useful to hear from other feminists and from persons who study male sexuality and aggression.

6.–7. There are no right answers to these questions.

8. She doesn't mention any. However, I don't see people changing their drinking behavior without some difficulty. I also find some difficulties in implementing other feminists' solutions; educating people takes time and money.

9. I'd like to discuss the class's emotional responses to Paglia's article. Did it make anyone mad? Did it make anyone laugh?

COMMENTS ON WRITING IDEAS

The first three writing ideas give students an opportunity to show that they have understood the basic steps of thoughtful decision making. These three ideas could be expanded by asking the student to refer to the process of thoughtful decision making described in the text in their evaluation of Wiley's, Turner's, Paglia's, and their own recommendations.

    The fourth writing idea asks students to describe their personal experience with conflict resolution. This idea could be expanded to ask the students to compare the process they used with the process of conflict resolution described in the text. The expanded writing idea would give students an opportunity to show their understanding of the process described in the text and to relate that process to their own personal experience.

The last writing idea can be used as a freewrite for class discussion when the class has finished reading the chapter.

CLASSROOM ACTIVITIES

Here are four sample classroom activities to develop skills in deciding how to act and in resolving a conflict.

Create a Talk Show

Description: Students volunteer to role-play the moderator and interested parties in a controversial decision. The remaining students play an active audience (asking questions and making points about the topic of discussion).

Possible talk show guests and topics:

a. Wendell Berry, Mrs. Berry, a computer manufacturer, a strip-mine coal worker, an "expert" on decision making, a surprise guest. *Topic:* Wendell's decision not to buy a computer.

b. Juli Loesch Wiley, Frederick Turner, a pregnant woman and her mate, a fetus, a baby, a zygote, a chicken awaiting the hatchet, God, and a surprise guest. *Topic:* What should a pregnant woman think about on the eve of an abortion?

c. Anita Hill, Clarence Thomas, Nancy Mitchell, a representative of "the majority of Americans," a surprise guest. *Topic:* What should a woman do when she has received unwanted sexual attention from her employer?

d. Camille Paglia, a fraternity man, a woman on the way to a fraternity party, a feminist, a college administrator, a surprise guest. *Topic:* What should we do to prevent date rape?

Purpose: To develop problem-solving skills

To develop ability to think creatively

To improve speaking skills

To learn steps in the process of thoughtful decision making

To develop an informed concern for contemporary social issues

To develop the capacity to listen to conflicting points of view

Conflict Resolution Role-play

Students divide into groups of three. They select two of the above interested parties and stage a disagreement between them. The third student acts as a moderator who guides the parties to do the following:

a. Take turns talking and listening to each other's points of view, including repeating back what the other said.

b. Try to resolve their dispute by exchanging reasons. If they disagree about the problem, ask them why they see the situation the way they do. If they disagree about their goals, ask them to describe the purposes for their goals, have them brainstorm alternative solutions, and ask them to consider whether one solution serves both their purposes (a win/win solution).

c. If they did not settle their disagreement by looking at each other's reasons, see if they can agree on a procedure for settling their disagreement.

d. If they agree to disagree, list the consequences of not resolving their disagreement. Are the consequences serious enough to send the disputants back to the bargaining table?

Purpose: To learn the steps of the process of conflict resolution

To develop the ability to think creatively

To improve listening skills

To develop respect for others

To develop the ability to give reasons for a position

To improve the ability to recognize consequences of action

Brainstorming Solutions

Description: The class selects a problem and brainstorms solutions, letting their imaginations range far and wide.

Purpose: To develop the ability to think creatively

To improve the ability to solve problems

Comparing Exercise Answers

Description: Students form groups to compare and contrast answers to selected exercises (not more than three or four examples at a time or not more than they can do in ten to fifteen minutes). The teacher moves from group to group checking on their progress and answering questions. The class reconvenes and reports answers they've found, noting the questions that have "right" answers and the ones that do not.

Purpose: To learn the steps of deciding how to act

To learn to identify unproductive shortcuts in thinking

To develop the ability to work productively with others

To develop creative thinking

QUIZ ITEMS AND ANSWERS

Items

Here are some items to select from when preparing your quizzes.

1. True/False

a. _____ The three steps in defining the problem are gathering the facts, analyzing the situation, and setting goals.

b. _____ Relevant facts are always obvious and so are easily gathered.

c. _____ When analyzing a situation, we are looking for causes.

d. _____ A moral dilemma occurs when two deeply held values come into conflict.

e. _____ When you are brainstorming, it's a good idea to critique ideas when they're first mentioned.

f. _____ Decision makers commit the fallacy of false dilemma when they assume they must take one of a given pool of alternatives when there are other, better ones if they look for them.

g. _____ It's a good idea to stick with what's available when deciding how to act.

h. _____ Because long-range effects are difficult to predict, you may as well ignore them when deciding how to act.

i. _____ You can always rely on nutshell briefings when gathering information about the pros and cons of proposed solutions.

j. _____ Going along with the group improves decision making.

k. _____ People commit the straw person fallacy when they criticize a person instead of criticizing the idea the person sets forth.

l. _____ If two people who dispute something aren't able to come up with a win/win solution, they can still find a way to resolve their conflict peacefully.

2. Are any of the following false alternatives? If so, list one or more additional alternatives to consider.

   a. If someone gives you unwanted sexual attention, you can either turn the person in to the authorities or ignore the situation.

   b. If your friends want you to steal something, you can either go along with them or tell them you do not approve of stealing.

   c. When a man insults you, you can either ignore him or sock him in the jaw.

   d. When someone offers you food you don't normally eat, you can either take it or decline to take it.

   e. If a customer asks for decaffeinated coffee and you don't have any left, you can either slip the customer decaffeinated coffee or explain that you don't have any decaffeinated coffee.

   f. When a student does poor work on a project, the teacher can either grade truthfully and demoralize the student or give the student a dishonest grade.

3. Short Answer

   a. The text lists three steps to take when defining a problem. What are they?

   b. The text lists four questions to ask yourself when reflecting on your goals. What are three of them?

c. The text lists four questions to ask yourself when sorting out the pros and cons of alternative solutions. What are three of them?

d. Describe possible advantages and disadvantages of taking one of the following shortcuts: Using what's available; the nutshell briefing. Use information from the text in your answer.

e. What is the straw person fallacy?

f. The text describes four different things people do when taking the shortcut of choosing from impulse. What are three of them?

g. The text describes two things you can do to hedge your bets against an uncertain future. What is one of them?

h. The text mentions two things you can do to help you understand someone who disagrees with you. What is one of them?

i. The text mentions a number of procedures to use for settling disputes. List three of them.

j. What is brainstorming, according to the text?

Answers

1. True/False

    a. True
    b. False
    c. True
    d. True
    e. False
    f. True
    g. False
    h. False
    i. False
    j. False
    k. False
    l. True

2. False Alternatives?

   a. There's another alternative. You could tell the person to leave you alone.

   b. There's another alternative. You can tell the person you have other plans. If you value honesty and do not approve of stealing, this is probably not a better alternative than one of the ones listed.

   c. You can tell the person not to talk to you in the tone of voice or with the words he or she is using.

   d. These look to me like the only two alternatives, though there are different things you could do with the food if you take it. You could take it and eat it or take it and feed it to the dog when no one's looking.

   e. You could go buy some, if there's a store around.

   f. The teacher could put no grade on the paper and give the student a chance to improve the paper for a grade. Or the teacher could put the low grade on the paper and give the student a chance to improve the paper.

3. Short Answer

   a. Gather the relevant facts, analyze the situation, set your goals.

   b. Any three of the following:

   What do I want to be different, and what would I like to keep the same about this situation?

   Do any of my goals matter more to me than others?

   Will any of my goals matter more or less to me in a different context?

   Are my goals *mine* or someone else's?

   c. Any three of the following:

   Will the proposed solution meet the goal you established?

   Will it have other, positive effects?

   Will it create any problems? Does it conflict with any of your personal or social values?

   What resources does the proposed solution use? Time? Money?

d. One of the following:

Using what's available: This shortcut saves time, but the best alternative may not be present in the available information. To find the best alternative, you may need to do some research or do some creativity exercises to discover other alternatives. Sometimes people commit the fallacy of false alternatives when they take this shortcut.

The nutshell briefing: This shortcut saves time, but when you rely on one person to report the pros and cons of possible solutions, you may end up with a slanted report. Sometimes nutshell briefers commit the straw person fallacy, presenting a weak version of a solution so they can knock it down easily.

e. People commit the straw person fallacy when they offer a weak version of a position or solution, criticize it, then conclude that the position or solution is not a good one.

f. Any three of the following:

"Me first:" Choosing the solution with the best outcome for oneself.

Retaliating: Acting from an angry impulse to punish rather than thinking through the pros and cons of using punishment to achieve the goal.

Avoiding punishment: Acting from fear of being punished with anger or insults by an authority or peer group instead of acting in accord with one's values.

Going along with the group: Suppressing a concern to avoid "rocking the boat."

g. One of the following:

Implement your decision in stages

Prepare contingency plans

h. One of the following:

Practice active listening

Seek a translator

i. Three of the following:

Take turns

Flip a coin

Agree to go with the advice of a trusted third party

Let the majority rule

j. To brainstorm, gather a group of people together, describe the problem, and invite everyone to call out any solution, no matter how zany. Do not critique or debate the solutions. Stay playful and nonjudgmental. Ask someone to record the solutions.

CHAPTER 3
BREAKING UP ARGUMENTS

This chapter teaches students how to break arguments into their parts and how to distinguish arguments from other kinds of exchanges that can occur in the general framework of the argument. These include communication enhancers, used to embellish parts of the argument, and support avoidance, used to distract listeners from the realization that speakers cannot support their point with evidence. Students learn to identify arguments, write arguments, and redirect disputes that aren't going anywhere. They also learn where to find arguments.

SUMMARY

This chapter defines "argument" as a statement or series of statements intended to support (establish, prove) another statement, and distinguishes argument from abuse and disagreement. Arguments are made up of conclusions, supports, and sometimes counterconsiderations.

The conclusion of an argument answers the question "What are you trying to show, establish, or prove?" Every argument has at least one conclusion, though it is not always stated. Many arguments contain a number of conclusions, some of which are subconclusions that support the argument's main conclusion (called a "thesis" in an argumentative essay). Some arguments have more than one main conclusion.

The following words are conclusion clue words: "thus," "therefore," "so," "consequently," "hence," "accordingly," "demonstrates that," "it follows that," "points to the conclusion that," "proves that," "gives us reason to believe that," "establishes," "justifies," "supports," "we can conclude that." Not all conclusions are introduced by conclusion clue words, and these words are sometimes used for purposes other than to introduce conclusions.

The main conclusion (thesis) of an argument is typically found toward the end of the first paragraph introducing the argument and again in the final paragraph of the argument. The word "conclusion" is ambiguous. It sometimes means "final" or "last." Other times, as in this chapter, it means a statement for which support is offered. Conclusions of arguments are not always last.

The support of an argument answers the questions "What do you have to go on to show, establish, or prove your conclusion?" and "How do you know that (what leads you to accept your conclusion)?" Support is offered for the main conclusion of an argument and the subconclusions of subarguments. Some arguments have unstated supports (also called "assumptions.")

The following are support clue words: "follows from," "in as much as," "after all," "as shown by," "for the reasons that," "may be inferred (deduced, derived) from," "for," "because," "since," "as indicated by." Not all support statements are introduced by support clue words, and these words are sometimes used for purposes other than to introduce supports.

Supports are generally found in the body of an argumentative essay, though one of the more interesting supports may also be stated in the introduction to capture audience attention. Sometimes there will be a paragraph early in the essay summarizing the supports the author will develop in the essay.

Counterconsiderations answer the question "What statement, evidence, or reason do you accept that goes against your conclusion?"

Decisions about what to do typically involve counterconsiderations. However, authors frequently omit counterconsiderations when presenting their reasoning to others, either because they rely on someone else to present the counterconsiderations or because they (advertisers, for example) hope to mislead their audience.

The following are counterconsideration clue words: "although," "even though," "in spite of (despite, notwithstanding)," "granted that," "on the one hand"; these introduce the counterconsideration. "But," "still," "yet," "on the other hand" and "more importantly" follow the counterconsideration and introduce the support statement the author offers to outweigh the counterconsideration. Not all counterconsiderations are introduced and followed by these words, and these words also perform functions other than introducing counterconsiderations.

Communication enhancers improve the communication of arguments. Some communication enhancers tell a joke or story or provide general background information (usually at the beginning of a speech or argumentative essay), define key terms in the argument, and elaborate the argument's conclusion. Though communication enhancers are important for communicating arguments, they do not provide support for the conclusion of an argument.

Support avoidance involves a shift away from giving support for the argument's conclusion by repeating oneself (loudly); abusing an audience through name calling, ridicule, and threat; or distracting an audience by interrupting the opposing speaker or changing the subject. Some of the activities common in support avoidance can also be used for enhancing communication, as when shouting is necessary because your audience can't otherwise hear you.

Some people thrive on support avoidance, and bystanders sometimes enjoy watching two argument makers "duke it out" using abuse and other such tactics on each other. Support avoidance, however, can be disconcerting at times. Some tactics for getting back on the support track include redirecting the conversation back to the exchange of support, making a joke about the support avoidance, or suggesting a break in the discussion to cool down.

You can expect to find written arguments in newspaper and magazine editorials, opinion pages, letters to the editor, movie and book reviews, scholarly and scientific journals, Supreme Court decisions, advertisements, and requests for contributions. You can expect to find oral (and written) arguments in contexts in which people are trying to figure out what happened and why, trying to decide how to evaluate something, and trying to decide how to act. Contexts that typically do not contain arguments include those intended to report or summarize events or findings or set forth definitions.

COMMON PROBLEMS FOR STUDENTS

Once again, language poses a problem for students. They hear the word "conclusion" and expect it to mean "last" or "summary statement." It takes a while before they get the idea that for a statement to be a conclusion in an argument it must stand in a certain logical relation to other statements.

Some students also have difficulty with the word "support." They assume that a statement must be true or acceptable to act as support, and so they refuse to identify a claim as support unless they accept the claim. They need to be reminded that an author can intend for a statement to serve as support, even if that claim is false. Of course, it's unlikely that an author would use a known false statement as support unless the author were trying to mislead an audience. But authors often accept claims—and offer them as support—that audiences do not accept. Thus the fact that an audience does not accept a claim does not prevent the claim from being support.

Often conclusions and supports aren't introduced with clue words, so readers must figure out the author's intention from the information available in the passage. But being able to figure out an author's intention itself presupposes that the reader understands how to make a reliable inference from sometimes sketchy information—a skill that students are still working on. Also, figuring out which sentences are good candidates for conclusions and which are good candidates for supports presupposes that the reader already has a solid understanding of what is being asserted when one asserts that something is the conclusion or the support of an argument. Because students are still grappling with the concept of the logical or evidential relation between claims, they sometimes have difficulty analyzing arguments.

Finding unstated support or assumptions also requires that students already have an advanced understanding of arguments. Although I mention unstated supports, I do not expect students to master finding unstated supports in this chapter, and I do not quiz them on this.

Finally, some students have difficulty identifying support avoidance, probably because they don't read the text carefully. Instead of looking for examples of audience abuse, interruption, or shouting, they select claims in need of support and for which no support has been given as examples of support avoidance.

I don't know of any magic cure for the difficulties students have analyzing arguments, but I believe it helps to recognize that argument analysis is no simple task. If you expect too much of your students too quickly you'll all end up frustrated. Take it easy and slow. You can continue working on the distinction between when something is and when it is not an argument as you discuss definitions and slanting with your students. And you can continue practicing argument analysis when you cover argument evaluation. Because I'm trying to make this text as practical as possible, I don't go into some of the fine points of argument analysis. You may want to supplement this text with additional material on argument analysis.

SAMPLE ANSWERS TO EXERCISES

Note: Strictly speaking, the clue words "so," "therefore," "because," and so on aren't part of the conclusions and supports. Also, to make the argument's structure evident, it's sometimes useful to paraphrase the conclusions and supports. Other times, direct quotes suffice. Finally, there is frequently more than one plausible way to answer the questions asked. Do not consider the answers suggested here as the final word.

1. a. *Main conclusion:* Either God isn't totally good or God doesn't cause everything.

   Subconclusion: None

   Conclusion clue word: So

   b. *Main conclusion:* No one can know whether or not they exist.

   Subconclusion: You have to see, hear, taste, touch, or smell something to know it exists.

   Conclusion clue word: So

   c. *Main conclusion:* You should believe that a god or goddess exists.

   Subconclusion: You'll be more likely to treat others well if you believe a god or goddess exists.

   Conclusion clue words: As a result.

   d. *Main conclusion:* People who believe in a male god should add a female god to their worship.

   Subconclusion: A male god gives men the hope that they can improve themselves spiritually but does little for women.

   Subconclusion: They should worship male and female gods.

Conclusion clue word: So.

e. *Main conclusion:* As far as virtue is concerned, Christ doesn't stand quite as high as some other people (Buddha and Socrates) known to history.

Subconclusion: There is one very serious defect in Christ's moral character and that is that He believed in hell.

Conclusion clue word: None.

2. a. *Mark's implied conclusion:* Dad should help me out with my phone bill.

Support: "I've had some unexpected expenses (tickets), and I'm short."

Dad's implied conclusion: I shouldn't help Mark with the bill.

Support: Our agreement was that if I paid for your tuition, books, and rent you would work and pay for the rest from your part-time job.

Dad's implied conclusion: You can impress your friend with your sense of humor and responsibility.

Support: That's how I impressed your mom.

Support clue word: None.

b. *Jorge's implied conclusion:* One of my roommates has been using my razor.

Support: It wasn't where I left it last time.

Juan's implied conclusion: I'm not the one who used it.

Support: There's a light hair on the razor.

Support and subconclusion: It's not mine.

Subsupport: My hair's as dark as yours, Jorge.

Tim's implied conclusion: I'm not the one who used it.

Support (and subconclusion): I'm not the only one with blond hair around here.

Subsupport: "Your new girl friend has blond hair, Jorge."

Support clue word: None.

c. Not an argument. This is an informational passage. It explains what the tenure system is.

d. *Support:* It's virtually impossible to fire someone with tenure, regardless of poor productivity.

Support: College professors should be judged by productivity, just like everyone else.

Support clue word: None.

e. *Conclusion:* The tenure system should continue.

Support and subconclusion: Administrators would be inclined to respond to public pressure and rehire only professors who espouse popular views if professors weren't protected with tenure.

Subsupport: Communities are more likely to donate funds to support ideas they agree with than ideas they disagree with.

Implicit subsupport: Universities need donated funds.

Support and subconclusion: Unpopular views should be taught.

Subsupport: The unpopular views of today are often the views that prepare us for tomorrow.

Support clue word: Since.

3. a. *Counterconsideration:* Lesbian and gay couples don't produce children who are biologically related to both members of the couple.

Response to counterconsideration: Neither do many heterosexual couples.

Counterconsideration clue words: Granted . . . but

b. *Counterconsideration:* We haven't graduated from college yet.

Counterconsideration clue words: True . . . but

c. *Counterconsideration:* I have been feeling a bit sick in the mornings . . .

Counterconsideration clue word: . . . but

d. *Counterconsideration:* College professors should teach unpopular views.

Counterconsideration clue words: Granted that . . . nonetheless . . .

e. No counterconsiderations are offered.

4. a. This passage does not contain an argument. It contains *communication enhancers.* It places the problem in historical context and explains the meaning of the phrase "comparable worth."

b. "The latest entry on the list of sacred democratic causes is comparable worth." This statement can be considered *support avoidance.* Rather than offering support for a conclusion, this statement attempts to belittle the doctrine of comparable worth by using the word "sacred" ironically.

The following sentences can be considered a *communication enhancer* as they serve to define the terminology being used. "According to that doctrine, it is demonstrable that low-paying female-dominated jobs, like nursing, are worth as much (to employers or society) as "comparable" male-dominated jobs, like plumbing, and that therefore by right and by law they should be paid the same."

The rest of the passage attempts to *enhance communication* by putting the doctrine in historical context—with a bit of *support avoidance* mixed in: "that sea of well-intentioned ambiguity and evasion." Here the author tries to make the supporters of comparable worth look bad—not giving reasons against the doctrine itself.

c. **Sue's conclusion:** You should wash the dishes.

   Support: I cooked dinner tonight.

   Support: We have an agreement to share kitchen chores.

   Jane's claims "I have done all the yard chores" and "I don't have time to do the dishes" are a form of support avoidance. Jane fails to address the issue of the agreement she has with Sue to share the kitchen chores. Because she has avoided this issue, her supports are a form of support avoidance (distracting the audience). She chooses to supply irrelevant statements in place of relevant support. In Sue's next statement, she addresses the fact that part of Jane's support is irrelevant to the argument at hand ("Both of us have homework. That's not the point") and then she restates her original support and conclusion ("We made an agreement to share the kitchen chores, and it's your turn"). Jane's reply is the form of *support avoidance* referred to as abusing the audience. ("You heartless bitch.")

   Finally, Sue is attempting to *refocus on support* by offering the option of both women doing their homework and then discussing the dishes.

d. Julie opens by stating her *conclusion* ("Now it's pay-back time.") and her *support* ("I've taken you out and showed you a good time.") These are both *elements of an argument.*

   Dave replies with a counterargument. His *conclusion* is "I don't owe you anything." And his *support* is that "You enjoyed yourself too."

   In her response, Julie practices *support avoidance (distracting the audience)* by ignoring Dave's counterargument and restating her own.

Finally, Julie resorts to *attacking her audience (support avoidance)* by threatening to spread rumors about Dave.

e. Stu opens with his *conclusion,* "You should drive to school today." This is an *element of an argument.*

Sid replies with a *counterconsideration:* "I prefer walking because it's more healthy." This is also an *element of an argument.*

Stu moves onto his *support,* "But if you drive you can do some errands we need." Support is an *element of an argument.*

SAMPLE ANSWERS TO READINGS FOR ANALYSIS

Jon Margolis, "Animals Have No Rights"

1. *Main Conclusion:* Unlike humans, animals have no rights (hereafter "C1").

   Margolis also argues for the conclusion (hereafter "C2") that humans have the responsibility to treat animals with kindness or at least without cruelty. (An alternative analysis would be to treat C2 as an elaboration on C1.)

2. *Supports:*

   a. *Support for C1.* Unlike humans, animals have no responsibilities. *Elaboration:* Animals have no moral responsibility.

      Subsupport: Animals face no moral choices. (The example of a hunting cat, for food and for sport, is used to support this subsupport.)

   b. *Support for C1 and C2.* Animals are dependent on humans.

   c. *Support for C1.* Rights accrue only to the independent.

      Subsupport: Only the independent can be responsible.

      Subsupport: All societies restrict the rights of dependent children.

      Subsupport: Animals are like forever dependent children.

   d. *Support for C2.* Animals have feelings.

3. *Counterconsideration:* Certain animals can be trained to exercise limited, operational responsibilities. The elaboration of (a) above is used to outweigh this counterconsideration.

4. *Communication enhancers:*

   a. The first three paragraphs are used to set up the essay that follows by offering information pertinent to the topic.

   b. The last five paragraphs elaborate on the argument's conclusions that animals do not have rights and that humans have the responsibility not to treat them cruelly.

5. *Support avoidance:*

   a. The author implies that if you don't agree that animals have rights, you're not a "true animal lover." He also dismisses furriers as motivated by greed.

   b. The author practices name calling: "Animal rightsniks."

6. Here's another question for discussion: How does Margolis define "rights"? Some of the support he offers works best for rights like the right to vote or serve on a jury, which require that one be a part of a moral community. It makes sense that dependent children and animals do not have these rights. But what about the right not to be injured or killed for human pleasure or convenience? It's not as clear that one need to be independent or a part of a moral community to have these rights. Also, I'd like to know how Margolis draws the cruelty line. He apparently thinks it is not cruel to separate and kill animals. I'd like to know more about why he thinks this.

Serge Etienne, "Rights for Animals"

1. *Main Conclusion:* Unstated: Margolis has not established that animals have no rights.

2. *Main supports with subsupports:*

   a. *Support:* Margolis is mistaken that responsibility is required for rights.

      Subsupport: Nonresponsible persons (infants, the mentally infirm, and comatose individuals) have been granted rights.

      Subsupport: Irresponsible persons (ones who have committed crimes) have rights.

   b. *Support:* You can't dismiss human cruelty to animals by calling attention to animal cruelty.

      Subsupport: Margolis is mistaken that chickens are cruel (intentionally and knowingly inflict pain on others without regard for their feelings).

Subsubsupport: Chickens do not peck each other to death from a preconceived plan but from overcrowding.

Subsubsubsupport: Chickens living in a reasonably natural environment are alert, vivaciously social, and courageous in protecting their young.

3. *Counterconsiderations:* I don't find any.

4. *Communication enhancers:* I don't find any.

5. Etienne claims that Margolis "shows his true feathers" when he writes that "Chickens are stupid . . . , etc." Etienne is questioning Margolis's motivations rather than looking at Margolis's reasons.

6. I'd like to see a discussion of the basis for granting rights. If, as Etienne argues, rights aren't assigned on the basis of responsibility, on what basis are they assigned? On what basis are babies and persons convicted of crimes assigned rights? Would this same basis serve for granting rights to animals?

Frances Byrn, "Death Penalty No Deterrent"

1. *Main Conclusion:*

   a. Not explicitly stated: America should abolish the death penalty. Many students offer "The death penalty is not a deterrent" because it's the title. Others offer "All killing is wrong," which comes toward the end of the article. Because the author doesn't provide evidence that all killing, including killing in war or self-defense, is wrong, I prefer the conclusion implied by what she does say.

2. *Main Supports:*

   a. The death penalty is not a deterrent.

   b. The death penalty has always been administered in a discriminatory fashion.

   c. Death penalty prosecutions also punish the families of the victims.

   d. After an execution, you cannot correct a wrongful conviction.

   e. Most countries look on the death penalty as a violation of human rights.

3. *Subconclusions and their support:*

   a. *Support:* The death penalty is not a deterrent.

   Subsupport: Many studies conducted have proved that the death penalty does not reduce the murder rate.

Subsupport: Studies in New York and California (when criminals were being executed in these states) show that the murder rate actually goes up with each execution.

b. *Support:* The death penalty has always been administered in a discriminatory fashion.

Subsupport: Studies have shown that the poor, uneducated, mentally retarded, and people of color are more likely to be sentenced to death.

Subsupport: Likewise, if the victim is white and middle or upper class, the death penalty is more likely to be given.

c. *Support:* Death penalty prosecutions also punish the families of the victims.

Subsupport: The long appeal process prevents the family from moving on with their lives.

Subsupport: The appeal process cannot be shortened without violating prisoner rights and without increasing the number of executions of innocent persons.

4. No counterconsiderations are stated. The author could admit that the death penalty does ensure that those who receive it will not murder again. The author could also admit that some families of victims do support the death penalty. They'd rather have the death penalty even if they do have to wait.

5. *Communication enhancers:* In the first paragraph and later in the article, Byrn puts the U.S. death penalty laws in context by comparing them with laws in other countries. (This can also be taken as support. We should abolish because other "democratic" countries have abolished it.)

6. *Support avoidance:* I didn't see any flagrant examples, though Byrn's use of the loaded term "bloodbath" could be considered support avoidance.

7. I'd like to discuss Byrn's use of the word "bloodbath." I'd also like to discuss the last sentence: "A judicial system based on revenge cannot do justice." What does Byrn mean by revenge? Is revenge the primary reason for capital punishment? Or is revenge the only thing left when deterrence is found inadequate to justify capital punishment? Is revenge unjust? In all forms?

Edward I. Koch, "Death and Justice: How Capital Punishment Affirms Life"

1. *Main Conclusion:* Not explicitly stated: The death penalty should not be abolished. (Stated: I support the death penalty.)

2.–3. *Main supports (subconclusions) with subsupports:*

   a. The death penalty helps to affirm that life is precious.

   Subsupport: Murderers such as Robert Lee Willie and Joseph Carl Shaw and Luis Vera would not have killed had they had the death penalty in mind at the time.

   Subsubsupport: When Willie and Shaw did have the death penalty in mind, they did realize that killing was wrong. On the eve of their executions they made statements that all killing is wrong, which implies that they found life precious then.

   Subsubsupport: Vera said that he knew he "wouldn't go to the chair" when he killed Rosa Velez.

   b. *Support* (not explicitly stated): The main arguments against the death penalty do not work. (These could also be considered counterconsiderations that Koch answers.)

   i. *Subsupport:* The fact that no other major democracy uses the death penalty does not indicate that the death penalty should be abolished here.

   Subsubsupport: "No other major democracy—in fact, very few other countries of any description—are plagued by a murder rate such as that in the United States."

   Subsubsupport: "If other countries had our murder problem, the cry for capital punishment would be just as loud as it is here."

   ii. *Subsupport:* Because the death penalty is applied in a discriminatory manner does not indicate that it should be abolished.

   Subsubsupport: The "lengthy and painstaking" appeals process minimizes the discrimination.

   Subsubsupport: Discrimination is a reason to extend the death penalty to other deserving persons, not to abolish it.

   iii. *Subsupport:* The proscription against killing in the Ten Commandments does not suffice to establish that capital punishment should be abolished.

Subsubsupport: The Torah specifies capital punishment for a variety of offenses.

   iv. *Subsupport:* The claim that the death penalty is state-sanctioned murder is confused.

     Subsubsupport: That's like calling legal imprisonment an act of kidnapping or calling taxation, extortion.

     Unstated Subsubsupport: It's confusing to say that legal imprisonment is kidnapping and that taxation is extortion.

     Subsubsubsupport: The state has rights and responsibilities the individual does not have.

  c. "When we protect guilty lives (by abolishing the death penalty), we give up innocent lives instead."

    Subsupport: "When opponents of capital punishment say to the state, "I will not let you kill in my name," they are also saying to murderers: "You can kill in your own name as long as I have an excuse for not getting involved.""

4. *Counterconsiderations:* "The death of anyone—even a condemned killer— diminishes us all." *Answer:* "But we are diminished even more by a justice system that fails to function."

5. *Communication enhancers:*

  a. The third paragraph serves as an introduction of Mr. Koch's qualifications as an authority.

  b. "The reasons I maintain my position can be best understood by examining the arguments most frequently heard in the opposition. . . . " This statement outlines what the author intends to do to provide support for his conclusion.

6. *Support Avoidance:*

  a. It's not clear how the fact that "the sixth of the Ten Commandments reads 'Thou shalt not commit murder'" can be used to establish religious support for capital punishment. Surely you don't have to find murder acceptable to reject capital punishment as the most effective or just way to respond to the problem of murder.

  b. Those who would call capital punishment "state-sanctioned murder" surely recognize that the state has some rights and responsibilities that individuals do not have. The question is whether the state has the right to kill. Koch's answer does not respond to these people.

c. I had difficulty deciding what to do with Koch's use of the Kitty Genovese example. He seems to think that not supporting the death penalty is tantamount to standing by and watching someone kill an innocent person. If so, then our horror at what happened to Kitty Genovese would lead us to accept the death penalty. If the two are not, as he thinks, equivalent, but are very different cases, then the Kitty Genovese example stirs up emotions that aren't directly related to the issue of capital punishment.

7. No suggested answer.

COMMENTS ON WRITING IDEAS

I've found that it's easier for students to write arguments that have supports and a conclusion than to find an argument elsewhere. Frequently they can write arguments with subarguments without understanding what they are doing—that is, they can't say how to analyze their arguments. If you ask students to bring in an argument and analyze it, you're asking them to do something more difficult than to write an argument and analyze it. In the second case, they're likely to start off with something that is an argument. However, when students go out looking for arguments, most of them come back with something else. Thus, the first writing idea is easier for students than the third idea—if you expect the student to come back with a letter that contains an argument.

The second and fifth writing ideas would make good freewrites for class discussion. The fourth writing idea is provided to help students realize that understanding argument analysis can help them with rewriting and editing.

CLASSROOM ACTIVITIES

Questioning Common Assumptions

Description: Call the students' attention to the "Your Thoughts about Arguments" exercise at the beginning of the chapter. Give them a minute to think about what "argument" means to them, then ask them to call out anything that comes to mind. Invite them to include any positive or negative associations they have to the word "argument." Write their answers on the board. Work with these ideas and the class to develop the distinction in the text between arguments and disputes. Discuss points of intersection between these categories. Notice that negative emotions are more likely to be associated with disputes than with arguments as a series of statements intended to support a conclusion.

Purpose: To recognize the ambiguity of the word "argument"

To develop emotional awareness

To develop analytic skills

To improve student ability to monitor their learning

Argument Analysis Clinic

Description: In this Argument Clinic, Communication Passages of various sorts, including Arguments, Communication Enhancers, and Support Avoiders, come into the waiting room. The Support Avoiders cannot be treated in the Clinic. They must be referred to Reform School. The Arguments are admitted into the Diagnosis and Treatment Area, and the Communication Enhancers are requested to wait in the waiting room to help the Arguments when they come out again.

To ensure that each entering Communication Passage is sent to the right place, a group of Pathology Interns study the Passages. The Pathology Interns dissect the passages into conclusions, support, counterconsiderations, communication enhancers, and support avoiders. They then present their findings to the Admissions Panel who double-check the Interns' work.

Students select short answer exercises or readings for analysis to review. Three students form the Admissions Panel, and the rest of the students divide into groups of Pathology Interns. The Pathology Interns work in groups dissecting the Passages. They then take their findings to the Admissions Panel for approval.

Purpose: To learn the concepts of argument analysis

To develop analytic skills

To develop the ability to apply concepts of analysis to new situations

To develop the ability to work productively with others

Cooling Down Hot Topics

Description: The class makes a list of hot topics and then forms into small groups. Each group picks a topic and writes a short conversation between two or more people who move back and forth among offering support, avoiding support, and using techniques (their own and those suggested in this chapter) to get back on track again. Afterward, the class discusses the pluses and minuses of the techniques used by the students' and suggested in the text for getting back on track.

Purpose: To develop the ability to apply to new situations the techniques learned for staying on track in an argument.

To develop analytic skills

To develop the ability to think creatively

To develop the ability to work constructively with others

To develop respect for others

To improve self-esteem and self-confidence

Comparing Exercise Answers

Description: Students form groups and compare and contrast answers to selected exercises (not more than one or two examples at a time or not more than they can do in 10 to 15 minutes). The teacher moves from group to group checking on their progress and answering questions. The class reconvenes and the groups report their answers, noting any confusion that emerged when they were trying to answer the questions.

Purpose: To develop the ability to apply concepts of argument analysis to new situations

To practice analytic skills

To learn to recognize and admit confusion

To learn to use time effectively

To learn to work productively with others

QUIZ ITEMS AND ANSWERS

Items

Here are some items to select from when preparing your quizzes.

1. True/False

   a. _____ An argument is a statement or series of statements that is intended to support another statement.

   b. _____ Arguments have only two main parts: conclusions and supports.

   c. _____ Supporting statements are never called premises.

   d. _____ The conclusion in an argumentative essay is called a thesis.

   e. _____ Counterconsiderations are statements the argument maker disagrees with.

   f. _____ "Because" introduces conclusions.

   g. _____ "Consequently" introduces conclusions.

   h. _____ Support statements are always introduced with support clue words.

   i. _____ Arguments sometimes begin with conclusions.

   j. _____ Sometimes an argument's conclusion is not explicitly stated.

2. Short Answer

   a. Name three parts of an argument.

   b. Name two types of communication other than the parts of arguments that are sometimes found in argumentative essays and conversations.

   c. The text lists four ways that argument makers enhance the communication of arguments. What are three of these ways?

   d. List four of the conclusion clue words listed in the text.

   e. List four of the support clue words listed in the text.

   f. Support for an argument that's not explicitly stated is called _____.

   g. What is a subargument?

   h. What is a counterconsideration?

    i. The text describes three main things that people do to avoid giving or receiving support for a conclusion. What are two of them?

    j. The text lists four ways to get back on the support track when someone's trying to derail you. What are two of them?

3. Some of the following passages are arguments; some of them are not. Indicate the arguments by underlining their main conclusions.

    a. This morning we found a seal cub lying on the beach. It looked at us with large, sad eyes when we walked toward it. Instead of being fat and sleek, it had deep folds in its skin.

    b. We found a seal lying on the beach that looked as though it were starving. It is probably an elephant seal cub because the park ranger said that elephant seals are weaning their cubs at this time of year. Some of the cubs aren't very good at catching fish for themselves and begin to starve when their mothers wean them.

    c. The seal we saw on the beach this morning looked listless and very thin. The seal will die unless it gets some help.

    d. Some people on the beach didn't care what happened to the seal; their footprints kept on going down the beach beyond where the seal was lying. If they cared about the seal, they would have turned around and walked back for help.

    e. We often see seals on the beach at the mouth of the Russian River. From a distance they look like rows of short fat pieces of driftwood. When they want something to eat they bounce across the sand and slither into the water, where their skin turns sleek and dark.

    f. Every event in the world is caused by some event prior to it. Either (a) the series of causes is infinite, or (b) the series of causes goes back to a first cause, which is itself uncaused. But an infinite series of causes is impossible. Therefore, a first cause, which is God, exists.[1]

    g. Humans are finite. God is infinite.

4. In the passages below underline the conclusions (including subconclusions), circle the first word of main conclusions, put a box around counter-considerations, and put x's through support avoidance.

---

[1] Donald Palmer, *Does the Center Hold? An Introduction to Western Philosophy* (Mountain View, CA: Mayfield, 1991) p. 192.

a. We'll probably have a good crop of apples this year. Granted, we had a poor crop last year, but we had heavy rain when the trees were blooming. The weather this spring was like the weather the year before last when we had a bumper crop. You're a fool if you think we're not going to have plenty of apples this fall.

b. Jose and Maria's arguments.

Maria:	You can't use the family car tonight . . .
Jose:	What, Mom? I've got to have the car.
Maria:	But . . .
Jose:	Come on Mom. I really need the car.
Maria:	Listen . . .
Jose:	I'm always listening to you. I want you to listen to me for a change. I need the car.
Maria:	Look, Jose . . .
Jose:	Mom, I mean it. I've got to have the car. There's this really cool girl I want to go out with.
Maria:	Jose . . .
Jose:	OK, then. It's OK?
Maria:	I'm sorry, Jose, your dad needs the car this evening. He's got an important business meeting across town.
Jose:	Why didn't you say so sooner?

c. Look, Dad, I know you want me to stop smoking. And I agree that smoking's not good for the lungs. But I shouldn't stop smoking until after I've finished finals. You see, I'm really nervous about getting through my finals. Lots of my friends got really nervous when they stopped smoking, so if I stop smoking I'll just get more nervous.

d. I don't know why you're being so stupid about hemp. Hemp fabric lasts longer than cotton, and it takes fewer pesticides to grow hemp than cotton, so farmers should raise hemp instead of cotton.

Answers

1. True/False

   a. True
   b. False; some arguments have counterconsiderations.
   c. False
   d. True
   e. False
   f. False
   g. True
   h. False
   i. True
   j. True

2. Short Answer

   a. Conclusion, support, and counterconsideration

   b. Communication enhancers and support avoidance

   c. Three of the following: background information, jokes or stories, definitions, elaborations of the conclusion.

   d. Four of the following: thus, therefore, so, consequently, hence, accordingly, demonstrates that, it follows that, points to the conclusion that, proves that, gives us reason to believe that, establishes, justifies, supports, we can conclude that.

   e. Four of the following: follows from, in as much as, after all, as shown by, for the reasons that, may be inferred (deduced, derived) from, for, because, since, as indicated by.

   f. Unstated support or assumption

   g. A subargument is a support statement (subconclusion) with its supports (subsupport).

   h. A counterconsideration is a statement that goes against an argument maker's conclusion.

   i. Any two of the following: repeat a disagreement (loudly), abuse an audience, distract an audience.

j. Any two of the following: go back to the last element of argument and begin again; jokingly agree with the attack and go back to the original point; ask the person to stop the support avoidance; suggest that you take a break until you're both ready to exchange support.

3. Indicate Arguments

   a. This is not an argument.

   b. *Conclusion:* It is probably an elephant seal cub.

   c. *Conclusion:* The seal will die unless it gets some help.

   d. *Conclusion:* Some people on the beach didn't care what happened to the seal.

   e. This is not an argument.

   f. *Conclusion:* A first cause, which is God, exists.

   g. This is not an argument.

4. Mark Conclusions and Others

   a. *Conclusion:* We'll probably have a good crop of apples this year.

      Counterconsideration: We had a poor crop last year.

      Support avoidance: You're a fool if you think we're not going to have plenty of apples this fall.

   b. *Jose's mom's main conclusion:* You can't use the family car tonight.

      Her subconclusion: Your dad needs the car.

      Jose's conclusion: I need the car.

      Support avoidance: Jose keeps interrupting his mother. He also keeps repeating himself.

   c. *Main conclusion:* I shouldn't stop smoking until after I've finished finals.

      Subconclusion: If I stop smoking I'll just get more nervous.

      Counterconsideration: Smoking's not good for the lungs.

   d. *Conclusion:* Farmers should raise hemp instead of cotton.

      Support avoidance: I don't know why you're being so stupid about hemp.

CHAPTER 4
DECIDING ON DEFINITIONS

This chapter teaches students how to identify, research, develop, and critique definitions so they can clarify language in argumentative papers and during conflict resolution. They can also use the information in this chapter for writing definition papers.

SUMMARY

Providing our audience with definitions helps them understand what we're saying. We offer definitions when words we use are ambiguous and our audience doesn't know which meaning we intend and when we're using a term that's new or unfamiliar to our audience.

Words can be defined in a number of different ways. Some of the most common are shown below.

Ostensive definition: In an ostensive definition, you show your audience what the word refers to.

Here's an ostensive definition of "book": A mother sitting by her child, pointing to the book in her hand, and saying "book."

Definition by example: In a definition by example, you list instances of the things the word refers to or tell a story that illustrates the meaning of the word.

Sometimes *negative* examples are useful; with these, you tell your audience what you do *not* intend the word to mean.

Here's a definition by example of "prejudice": A Cambridge University student said, "I despise all Americans. But," he added, a bit puzzled, "I've never met one that I didn't like."

Connotative definition: A connotative definition identifies common characteristics of the things the word refers to. Many dictionary definitions are connotative definitions.

It is sometimes useful to identify the connotative definition you will use for a word to distinguish it from other connotative definitions that your audience might use for the same word.

Here's a connotative definition of "prejudice": "Prejudice" means thinking ill of others without sufficient warrant.

Definition by synonym: A definition by synonym lists a word or words that have roughly the same meaning as the word being defined.

Here's a definition by synonym for "prejudice": "Prejudice" means roughly the same as "bigotry," "intolerance," and "narrow-mindedness."

Definition by metaphor: A definition by metaphor defines something by equating it with something different.

Here's a metaphorical definition of "prejudice": Prejudice is the lock that keeps a closed mind shut.

Expressive definition: An expressive definition sets forth the evaluation and/or feelings or emotions people express or experience when they use, read, or hear words.

Here's an expressive definition of "prejudice": "Prejudice" expresses and evokes disapproval and negative emotions such as anger and fear.

Definition by association: A definition by association sets forth the thoughts, feelings, images, and evaluations that come to mind when one hears a word. Frequently different people have different associations for a word, even when they agree on the word's connotative definition. Often the associations are stereotypes that are not generally true of the group of people or things the word refers to.

Here's a definition by association of "prejudice": Some associations people have with "prejudice" are feelings of inferiority, unfair laws, anger, being despised, insults, fights.

There are many books to consult when researching definitions, including the giant *Oxford English Dictionary* and specialized dictionaries, such as *The Bias-Free Word Finder*. Etymological dictionaries that tell a word's origin may not capture your meaning of a word but may provide some interesting alternatives to contrast with your meaning.

When you consult a dictionary that offers several meanings of a word, you need to select a definition that most closely describes what you are talking about. Because language changes quickly and because dictionaries typically record the meanings of published words, many words and meanings are not recorded in dictionaries. Books and articles on a specific topic also frequently contain definitions of key terms of the topic. You can develop your own definitions by telling stories from your experience to develop story examples, by using analytic skill to find similarities among specific examples to develop connotative definitions, and by using your imagination to develop metaphorical definitions.

The following are some questions to ask when critiquing definitions:

1. Is the definition vague or circular?

2. Did the definition ignore a useful distinction? Is the same definition given for two words that could potentially mean different things?

3. Was the definition appropriately broad or narrow? Was it too broad, including instances that you wanted to exclude? Was it too narrow, excluding instances that you wanted to include?

COMMON PROBLEMS FOR STUDENTS

Some students have difficulty distinguishing the different types of definitions. When developing definitions, students have the most trouble finding connotative definitions and illustrating them with story examples. When students write story examples, these tend not to be specific enough, and students have difficulty finding the similarities among the examples to develop a connotative definition. I also find that students aren't very attentive to subtle differences in meaning; if you ask them to compare and contrast two connotative definitions for the same word, they will often find no differences when there are some. In short, many students have weak analytic and language skills, so it's worth spending some time with definitions to address these weaknesses.

SAMPLE ANSWERS TO EXERCISES

1. a. *Connotative definition:* This definition describes common features of houses.

   b. *Metaphorical definition:* This definition compares a house to a trap.

   c. *Definition by synonym*

   d. *Definition by examples*

   e. *Connotative definition:* This definition describes something the author considers common to just laws—namely, that they are arrived at by the full participation of everyone who will be governed by the law.

f. *Connotative definition:* This definition describes a common feature of laws, namely, that they are rules that carry a penalty if not followed.

g. *Definition by example:* This definition gives two specific examples of the sorts of things the definition maker means by "law."

h. *Definition by example:* This definition tells a story to illustrate success.

i. *Connotative definition:* This definition describes something the author considers a common feature of successes.

2. a. The example is adequate for the definition given; the cousin's decision to date is based on the race of those he is interested in. However, the definition as stated is broader than the way we commonly use the word "racism." "Racism" is usually used to describe a practice one believes is wrong. We could make this connotative definition more explicit by adding that the decision is made unjustly on the basis of race. Whether a person would consider the cousin's behavior an example of racism, according to the revised definition, depends on whether the person believes that it's wrong to date only members of one's own ethnic group. Some people may consider this practice a way of denigrating other races. Others may not.

b. The example is inadequate for the definition given; the two roommates do not share the same values. Also, the definition is too narrow; families do not necessarily share the same values.

c. Whether one takes this example to be adequate depends on how one interprets the phrase "primary residence." Jail is Jill's primary residence in the sense that she doesn't go anywhere else to stay the night. On the other hand, if she's in jail only temporarily, then her primary residence could be the place she lived before and will return to after jail. If the example stated that Jill was in jail for life with no parole option, then jail would be her primary residence. In any case, the definition of home as primary residence leaves out the emotional connections that people have with their homes.

d. The example is adequate for the definition given. However, the definition is very narrow.

e. The example is adequate for the definition given.

3. The stories are examples of acquaintance rape. Bob admitted to ignoring Patty's protests, and Patty admitted to giving up the struggle when she felt threatened. This is rape. The stories show how the people involved can have very different ideas about what's happening and illustrate why we need to have more successful

communication about sex. The consequences of unsuccessful communication are severe.

4. a. The definition has an element of circularity. "Race" needs to be defined.

   b. *Vague.* Further definition of "getting ahead" is needed for this definition to be clear.

   c. *Circular.* This calls for the use of terms other than "lacking security."

   d. *Not vague or circular.*

   e. *Vague.* There must be more to health than not being ill.

5. a. Ignores the distinction between the words "gender" and "sex." One is cultural (gender), the other anatomic/biological (sex).

   b. No noted lack of distinction

   c. The second definition fails to make a distinction between jealousy and envy.

   d. No noted lack of distinction

6. a. The broadest definition of "sexism" is the first one. An example would be, "Cindy choose John to date because he is a man and she's heterosexual."

   b. The broadest definition of "family" is the third one. "Even though we are not related by blood, I feel that Sara is my sister. Her father is my nanny and they have lived with us for several years."

   c. The broadest definition of "home" is the first one. "Although we only spend our summers in the cabin, it sure does feel like home."

   d. The broadest definition of "success" is the first one. "I feel successful when I just finish weeding the garden!"

   e. The broadest definition is the second one. "My mentor at school helps to keep me disciplined with my school work." (Some people may understand the second definition to be limited to accepting the authority or control of *others*. In that case, it covers a different class of actions, not a broader class of actions.)

7. a. *Broader:* "Love is a feeling one person has for another."

      Narrower: "Love is an intense pleasurable feeling between a husband and wife."

   b. *Broader:* "An American is someone who lives in North, Central, or South America."

      Narrower: "An American is someone who was born in the United States."

c. *Broader:* "Health is a state of biological function."

   Narrower: "Health is the absence of disease and the presence of a positive attitude."

d. *Broader:* "A friend is someone you know."

   Narrower: "A friend is someone you know better than anyone else, someone you are fond of, and someone who comes to your aid in times of trouble."

e. *Broader:* "Trust is belief in another person's honesty."

   Narrower: "Trust is the firm belief in a friend's honesty."

8. a–d. There are no right answers to these exercises.

SAMPLE ANSWERS TO READINGS FOR ANALYSIS

Ellen Goodman, "Sexual Bullying in Schools"

1. Example (the opening stories), connotative (the definition in paragraph 5), and metaphor ("Sexual harassment is an older cousin to bullying")

2. There is no right answer to this question.

3. The definition "unwanted and unwelcome sexual behavior which interferes with your life" is vague. In what way does the unwelcome behavior interfere with a person's life? Depending on how "interfere" is interpreted, the definition would be broader or more narrow. It would be useful to compare this definition of sexual harassment with definitions provided by your college campus. Sometimes different degrees of unwanted attention are described with different disciplinary implications. Students should understand these differences.

4. There are no right answers to this question.

5. Your opinion is asked for here.

6. That students should call attention to it when it happens and express their disapproval. That schools teach respect and courage.

7. Your opinion is asked for here.

8. There are no right answers to this question.

Peter Schrag, "Bias, Harassment Reports out of Focus: Girls Shortchanged?"

1. He criticizes the AAUW's definition by saying, ". . . any nasty remark and a great deal of childish thoughtlessness was evidenced of sexual harassment . . ." In other words, he thought the definition was too broad. He lists some examples, but he does not quote the connotative definition.

2. Your opinion is asked for here.

3. Your opinion is asked for here.

4. There is no definition of sexual harassment offered in the body of this article.

5. A policy of "civility and mutual respect." As he blames the problem on the deterioration of "the power of schools to enforce reasonable codes of civil behavior," perhaps he thinks that schools should be permitted to enforce behavior codes. He encourages authorities to control student behavior. Goodman's policy in the previous article implies that students can influence each other.

6. Your opinion is asked for here.

Jack Forbes, "Only Approved Indians Can Play: Made in the U.S.A."

1. A true Indian is at least one-quarter Indian blood and has a Bureau of Indian Affairs (BIA) roll number.

2. Your opinion is asked for here.

3. No. This story is written with an ironic tone. I'd say that Forbes is asking us to question this definition of "Indian." I'd say that Forbes would like us to think about the other possible defining characteristics, such as language and political integrity (the Tarahumara tribe "resisting the Mexicanos"). Even so, I'm not sure what Forbes would give as a definition of "Indian," but I believe he doesn't want the BIA or other U.S. government officials providing the definition.

4. Your opinion is asked for here.

5. Your opinion is asked for here.

COMMENTS ON WRITING IDEAS

The first writing idea gives students a chance to practice the analytic skills they have so much trouble with. Though they have difficulty with this assignment, they are glad to do it, especially if they are allowed to select words to define that are special in some way to them. The third and fourth writing ideas also give students practice using analytic skill.

The second writing idea is a good one for an ungraded freewrite. Students should let their imaginations soar with this one. The sixth writing idea is also a good one for a freewrite for class discussion. The fifth writing assignment gives students practice incorporating definitions in arguments.

CLASSROOM ACTIVITIES

Story Example Skits

Description: Students select words that can be defined with story examples. Then they form groups, develop skits, and perform their skits for each other. The class as a whole develops connotative definitions that fit the skits. Some words to consider include assertive versus aggressive, altruistic versus selfless, arrogant versus confident.

Purpose: To develop the ability to apply definitional concepts to new situations

To develop analytic skills

To develop the ability to think creatively

To develop the ability to work productively with others

To practice having fun when learning

Creating Metaphors Competition

Description: Students try to stump each other developing metaphorical definitions of words. The class selects two lists of words to define metaphorically and divides into two groups. Each group has five minutes to select a list of ten things that the other group must use to create metaphorical definitions. Then each group takes ten minutes to develop as many metaphorical definitions as they can think of, using the list given them. The class as a whole discusses how to evaluate the definitions to select the best ones.

Purpose: To develop the ability to think creatively

To learn how to develop and assess metaphorical definitions

Short Oral Presentations

Description: Students make brief (less than two minutes) oral presentations defining a word that has some special significance to them. They provide visual, tactual, musical, or olfactory aids as a focal point of their presentations. No reading is allowed. After each presentation, students in the audience take turns giving the presenter specific, positive feedback. The audience also identifies the type of definition that was given: metaphorical, connotative, example, ostensive, some combination, and so on. In addition, the audience indicates whether the definition is broader or narrower or in other ways different from how they understood the word defined.

Purpose: To develop analytic skills

To improve speaking skills

To apply definitional concepts to new situations

To develop self-confidence

To develop respect for others

To clarify one's own values

Definition Debates

Description: The class selects a passage or reading from the text that contains a controversial definition. They then divide into two groups. One group develops arguments in favor of the definition. The other group develops arguments against it. The class reconvenes and the teacher moderates the debate.

Purpose: To practice critiquing definitions

To practice giving reasons for conclusions

To improve speaking skills

To learn the social consequences of definition selection

QUIZ ITEMS AND ANSWERS

Items

Here are some items to select from when preparing your quizzes.

1. True/False

a. _____ An ostensive definition is a definition that contains large words.

b. _____ Some definitions by example tell stories.

c. _____ "Prejudice is being down on someone you're not up on" is an example of a connotative definition.

d. _____ Synonyms mean exactly the same thing.

e. _____ Definitions by metaphor awaken the imagination.

f. _____ Expressive definitions list associations people have with words.

g. _____ "Connotations" sometimes means "associations."

h. _____ Etymological dictionaries provide word origins.

i. _____ A good college dictionary contains all the words that college students use.

j. _____ Developing definitions requires analytic skill and imagination.

k. _____ Vague definitions are imprecise.

l. _____ Dictionaries sometimes use circular definitions to save space.

m. _____ It's always more appropriate to use a narrow definition than a broad one.

n. _____ The scope of a definition has to do with how many words the definition contains.

o. _____ We use counterexamples to show that a definition is inappropriately broad or narrow.

2. Identify the types of definitions below.

   a. Yesterday Jane shouted obscenities at her father when he said she couldn't use the car. That's what I mean by "aggression."

   b. Today when Juanita's father said he decided not to let her use the car because he wanted to go to his club meeting, she told him that she was disappointed in his decision because it meant that she wouldn't be able to get to her night class. That's what I mean by "assertion."

   c. Aggression is abusive verbal or physical behavior.

   d. Assertion is clearly stating one's needs and opinions.

   e. Aggression is the fuel for the fire of conflict.

   f. Assertion is the path to mutual understanding.

   g. "Aggression" evokes negative judgments and emotions such as fear and anger.

   h. "Assertion" either evokes no strong emotions or judgments or evokes mildly positive ones.

3. Do the following examples fully illustrate the following definitions? Explain. Do any of the examples lead you to question whether the definition is too broad or too narrow to explain the meaning of the word, as you understand it? Explain.

   a. *Definition:* Aggression is violent behavior.

      Example: Kim's pushing Lee out of the way so Kim could get in the checkout line is an example of aggression.

   b. *Definition:* Health is not having an illness.

      Example: My skiing friend, Jake, doesn't have an illness, but he did just break his leg.

   c. *Definition:* Peace is the absence of violent conflict.

      Example: Manny's parents have stopped their physical attacks on each other. Now they just live in quiet desperation.

   d. *Definition:* Indoctrination is inculcating beliefs in others by repetition instead of by giving reasons.

      Example: My little sister came to believe that "proboscis" means nose because I said "proboscis" to her over and over when pointing to her nose.

4. Rewrite the following definitions to make them broader, then narrower.

   a. Music is sound with rhythm.

   b. Being judgmental is having the disposition to state one's negative opinions.

5. Is any of the following definitions vague or circular or does it fail to maintain a useful distinction? Explain.

   a. "Aggression" means assertion.

   b. "Assertion" means asserting oneself clearly.

   c. "Support" means a statement that's offered to support another statement.

   d. "Shy" means reserved.

Answers

1. True/False

   a. False
   b. True
   c. True
   d. False
   e. True
   f. False
   g. True
   h. True
   i. False
   j. True
   k. True
   l. True
   m. False
   n. False
   o. True

2. Identify Definitions

   a. Definition by example
   b. Definition by example
   c. Connotative definition
   d. Connotative definition
   e. Definition by metaphor

   f. Definition by metaphor
   g. Expressive definition
   h. Expressive definition

3. Illustrate Definitions

   a. This example does fit the definition. Pushing someone out of the way is violent behavior.

   b. This example does fit the definition. A broken leg is not an illness, like measles or chicken pox. However, this example does lead me to question the definition of health. I would want a person with a broken leg to get health care, for example. The definition of health given is too narrow to include the broken leg.

   c. The example does fit the definition. The parents aren't engaging in violent conflict. However, this example leads me to question the definition of peace. It's too narrow to include the emotional disease between Manny's parents.

   d. The example does fit the definition. It leads me to question the definition. I usually think of indoctrination as something negative, as when advertisers uses repetition to trick us into false expectations about their products. I'd want a definition of indoctrination that rules out teaching language as an example of indoctrination. The definition is too broad for my purposes.

4. Broader/Narrower Definitions

   a. *Broader:*   Music is sound.

      Narrower: Music is sound with rhythm and pitch.

   b. *Broader:*   Being judgmental is having the disposition to state one's opinions.

      Narrower: Being judgmental is having the disposition to state one's negative opinions loudly and on every possible occasion.

5. a.   The definition clouds the distinction between violent and nonviolent expressions of wants and needs.

   b. This definition is circular.

   c. This definition is circular.

   d. This definition clouds the distinction between being unlikely to open up with strangers and being unlikely to open up at all.

CHAPTER 5
ATTENDING TO LANGUAGE

This chapter introduces some primary types and effects of language to help students select language for precise and engaging communication and to help them avoid being misled and controlled by others.

SUMMARY

Ambiguity undermines communication when the audience doesn't know which meaning is intended. Ambiguity enhances communication when the ambiguity is used to say more with less or to intrigue.

When we use irony we say the opposite of what we mean as a way to express (mild) criticism. Irony is often humorous. Audiences sometimes have trouble telling whether words are meant ironically. Contextual clues, background information about the author, and outrageous or clearly unacceptable claims provide clues of an ironic message.

Advertisers use modifiers that weaken claims ("help," "may") along with strong-sounding language ("guarantee") to make weak claims that look strong. In such a context the modifiers that weaken claims are called "weasel words." Advertisers also use words like "new," which sound good but mean very little. An advertiser can make some minor change in a product and label it "new." Once again, the claim looks strong but is in fact weak.

Writers use metaphors and vivid descriptions to awaken the reader's senses. Metaphorical language identifies one thing with another quite different thing. Lively metaphors evoke images. Tired, repeatedly used metaphors do not. In either case, metaphors affect how we think, sometimes revealing and sometimes concealing things we should know. Tired metaphors become more lively when extended.

Vivid descriptions use concrete and sensory words. They capture audience attention because they evoke sensory images. Pallid descriptions use general terms and abbreviations. They distance and sometimes mislead an audience, but they are useful for summarizing and making general claims.

Some words ("terrorist," "freedom fighter") describe and express evaluations and emotions. People select labels that make the actions of those they support sound good and the actions of those they disagree with sound bad. To avoid being misled by expressive language, make sure authors supply sufficient evidence to support the emotions and evaluations their words express.

Gordon Allport introduced the phrase "labels of primary potency" to describe general terms for groups that carry stereotypes with them ("deaf," "Mexican"). Labels of primary potency distort our perceptions of individuals unless we do something to shed the stereotypes. Language that promotes stereotypes ("victim," "lady doctor," "male ego") also distorts our perceptions of individuals.

We can shed stereotypes by replacing gender-specific language with gender-neutral language ("doctor" not "lady doctor"), by turning a label of primary potency into an adjective ("Mexican college professor" not "Mexican"), by dropping the label (stop using "girl" for woman), and by changing the label ("African American" instead of "Negro"). To permanently prevent labels from taking on stereotypes, we need to stop thinking in terms of stereotypes altogether.

COMMON PROBLEMS FOR STUDENTS

With some guidance, students readily recognize the different types of language used by others. They have more difficulty incorporating these language lessons in their own writing. They tend to write in general terms—especially when they don't know much about the topic—instead of using specific, detailed, concrete examples to illustrate a definition or support a claim. They also tend to move back and forth between evaluating and describing without being aware of what they're doing. And they have difficulty producing examples of playful ambiguity to enliven their paper titles and introductions. It's important therefore to give students practice working with their own writing so they do not merely become adept in recognizing different types of language used by others but can use language successfully themselves.

SAMPLE ANSWERS TO EXERCISES

1. a. This person is using irony to make a point against censorship on the Internet. The statement, "How much better it is for them to watch tens of thousands of natural images of murder and mayhem on television and in the movies," sums up the irony.

    b. Deliberate ambiguity using the two different definitions for the word "recession": the economic recession and the receding hairline. One implication is that you'll do better economically if you have a full head of hair.

    c. Misleading weasel words occur throughout this ad. Consider, for example, "Free opportunity kits." This ad is trying to sell training programs. They're not likely to give all their secrets away in the "free" kit. Consider also, "Foley-Belsaw's unique training programs can make those dreams come true!" The advertiser hopes the reader will take this to mean that the training programs *will* make the dreams come true, but the statement doesn't say this. Also, note the language in "you can earn as much as $49.94 for a simple tune-up." Once again it doesn't say you *will* earn anything and certainly not that you will earn $49.94. You will only earn "as much as" that. Perhaps you will earn considerably less.

    d. Deliberate ambiguity; the word "pot" has two meanings: marijuana and ruin.

2. a. "Mainstream" is a metaphor used to compare thought or opinion with the strongest or main current in a river. It's a misleading metaphor here. Republican thinking is hardly a mainstream of Black American thought.

    b. Vivid description

    c. Pallid description. This could be anything from a broken fingernail to a death in the family.

    d. Tired metaphor. We have heard this one again and again.

    e. The word "impressed" slides over the fact that these men were taken against their will and forced to fight in wars of a country of which they are no longer citizens. This is an example of pallid description.

    f. Lots of metaphors: "kicking," "habit of drug prohibition," "siphoning off the resources," "brushed off like a piece of lint." Some are more lively than others. I didn't notice "siphoning" at first; it's used so frequently it didn't stand out as a metaphor. The metaphor of drug prohibition as addiction is quite lively.

    g. Lively metaphor: "Bread turns me into a Ferdinand the Bull."

3. There are no right answers with regard to the rewritten language. The following will focus on words that perpetuate stereotypes and positive/negative words.

    a. "Let freedom ring" is a positive phrase that supports the stereotype of the United States as a place where all are free.

    b. The words "plus-size," and "large-size" are positive words. So is "thrifty gene."

    c. In a democracy where "the majority rules," calling groups "minorities" implies that their views need not become public policy. Also, repeated attention to a difference in numbers of African Americans, Asian Americans, or Mexican Americans compared with European Americans also distracts from looking for similarities that exist among these groups. The phrase "underrepresented group" works better to make the point that some groups whether minorities or not (women, for example, are not minority groups) have less political and economic power than their numbers might imply. Other minority groups (wealthy white males) have more political and economic power than groups of a comparable size.

d. The words all promote stereotypical images. They're also metaphors. Man as meat; woman as animal or clothing.

e. This entire passage promotes the stereotype of the layperson not understanding scientific information. It contrasts antivivisectionists with scientists, implying that no antivivisectionists are scientists.

f. This quotation compares Japanese Americans to snakes to support the distrust of Japanese Americans during the second world war.

4. a. Although he started out by referring to "human events," Jefferson consistently refers to "mankind" and "Men," removing women from the list of Americans who are created equal. He also uses evaluative language that sounds very important "Laws of Nature and Nature's God," "unalienable Rights," and "Life, Liberty and the pursuit of Happiness" and "just powers," and serves to make his cause sound honorable.

b. Mencken uses double negatives to create an almost indecipherable editorial. His use of stereotypical "country folk" language adds to the possibility that his words will be ignored and to the stereotype of this population as uneducated.

c. Ms. Dodd uses vivid description (five feet ten inches high, round shouldered, thick lips, complexion and hair dark, gray eyes, . . .), negative words ("swindler," "villain"), and lively metaphor (go to the devil) in her warning.

d. Kush uses metaphors, some of which also promote stereotypes (calling the police "piggies" and "you are what you eat," "choppered-up to be"), vivid description ("swooped down with their helicopter"), irony ("most evil of weeds," "chopper of justice," "stalwart CAMP cops," "upholders of justice," "protectors of peace and justice").

5. a. "Soar without leaving the ground": metaphor and positive sounding; "help launch careers," "can choose," "fields that can get," "can get college credits": weasel words; "future moving forward—fast": positive sounding; "future up in the air": metaphor, ambiguity (uncertain future or future in the air force) and negative or positive sounding; "best opportunities": positive sounding.

b. "Our engineers have spent the last 28 years polishing it": deliberate ambiguity; "trust and confidence," "perfecting," "customer satisfaction," "innovative," "trustworthy": positive sounding words; perfecting Corolla for over 28 years:

deliberate ambiguity that's potentially misleading for it gives the impression that the Corolla you purchase will be as perfect as it would be if someone had been perfecting it for 28 years; "available integrated child safety seat": a bit weasely as the small print footnote indicates that it's optional only on the DX model; "almost like having a Toyota mechanic": also a weasel expression.

SAMPLE ANSWERS TO READINGS FOR ANALYSIS

Mark Twain, "The War-Prayer"

1. *Vivid description:* "organ burst that shook the building," "An aged stranger . . . moved with slow and noiseless step, eyes fixed on the minister, long body clothed in a robe . . . unnaturally pale face." *Effects:* This answer will vary from person to person. I hear the organ and see the stranger. I feel present in the church. "Shrieks of their wounded," "writhing in pain." *Effects:* This answer will vary from person to person. I almost feel the pain.

   Metaphorical language: "country up in arms," "in every breast burned the holy fire of patriotism."

   Irony: "holy fire," "glad and gracious time," "the half dozen rash spirits," "We ask in the spirit of love, of Him Who is the Source of Love." *Effects:* This answer will vary from person to person. My emotions are mixed when I read it; it's dark humor, frightening and humorous.

2. *Metaphor and irony.* See above.

3. The story is an exaggerated account of patriotism and uses generalizations, such as "in every breast," which even in the story is contradicted with "half dozen rash spirits that ventured to disapprove." The story would have to be completely rewritten, adding details of how patriotic people often have mixed feelings about war.

4. Yes, he does. Though much of it is used ironically—"holy fire," for example. Twain puts many positive sounding words into the first prayer: "ever-merciful and benignant Father," "noble young soldiers," "patriotic work," "shield them," "invincible." He puts more vivid descriptions and negative sounding words into the second prayer: "bloody shreds," "desolated land in rags and hunger and thirst."

5. Twain's main point is that sometimes people get carried away with patriotism and don't think through the effects of their actions. The language of patriotism disguises reality. Even when patriots are told what their words mean, they are so carried away that they will not listen.

6. There is no right answer to this question.

Ronald Reagan, "President's Speech to U.S. after Bombing Libya"

1. *Vivid descriptions:* There aren't many. Reagan talks in fairly general terms even about the "terrorist" bomb exploding in the nightclub. He tells the reader that two people were killed and 230 others wounded, but he doesn't paint a vivid picture of how they were killed or wounded. His language describing the U.S. military action is even more pallid. He says the United States "launched a series of strikes against the headquarters." That language evokes no specific sensory images.

   Metaphorical language: "their country a synonym for barbarism," "caught in the grip of a tyrant," "salute the skill."

   Ironic: None, though the informed audience might find Reagan's outrage at terrorism ironic given that he supported the Contras who used terrorism to destabilize the Nicaraguan government.

2. Calling Khadafy's government a "regime," and using the expression "reign of terror" imply that Khadafy's government has no positive qualities.

3. The word "terrorist" is used repeatedly. A terrorist is someone who uses violence (often against "innocent bystanders") for political purposes. What it expresses and what's associated with it will vary from person to person. However, it typically expresses fear and disapproval and is associated with bombs, screams of pain, buildings crashing down, the IRA, Israel, and Palestine. The effect of using "terrorist" repeatedly is to get the audience to have strong negative associations with Khadafy and to support the United State's violent attack on Libya.

   Reagan uses positive-sounding words to describe the United State's violent response: "succeeded in their mission." A mission is an assigned task. It's associated with honorable intentions: "the mission statement of the university," "missionaries." Reagan expects it to evoke feelings of hope and approval in the general audience. For audiences who have suffered the effects of paternalistic missionaries and misguided missions, "mission" may evoke contempt or distrust.

4.–5. There are no right answers to these questions.

Alexander G. Higgins, "2 Pilots Destroy Record 23 Tanks"

1. The article doesn't create a detailed picture of the effects of "hitting tanks." It's almost possible to read the story and doubt that any person was harmed.

2. To begin with, the Fourth of July is a U.S. holiday so I wouldn't expect an Iraqi to use that expression. But even if the expression were familiar, I would not expect an Iraqi to compare the burning death of a loved one to celebratory fire works. The metaphor conceals the human suffering occasioned by the "fireworks."

3. I would describe the persons in the tanks and how "killing the tanks" affected them.

Richard Cohen, "'White Male' Resents Term"

1. The stereotype that all white males have economic and political power and are responsible for the problems of society

2. He describes his father who was "born in poverty, raised in an orphanage, retired on a paltry pension and Social Security."

3. Negative sounding. In the past, being called "white" was positive sounding, as in the expression "free, white, and 21."

4. The main point is to get the reader to question lumping all white males together as equally politically and economically powerful. Seems like a good idea to me.

5. There are no right answers to this question.

COMMENTS ON WRITING IDEAS

The first writing idea asks students to rewrite something they've already written. It reinforces the notion that rewrites are a part of the writing process. It also gives students practice paying attention to and improving ambiguity, metaphors, vivid and pallid descriptions, expressive language, and language that evokes stereotypes in their own writing.

The second writing idea gives students the opportunity to practice writing irony. It would make a good freewrite for class discussion. The third writing idea focuses on using language to mislead. It would also make a good classroom freewrite, as would the fifth writing idea. The fourth writing idea asks students to write an argument about language use. Students could write about this, then stage debates in class on the topic.

CLASSROOM ACTIVITIES

Removing Distance with Vivid Language

Description: The class divides into groups, and each group rewrites a section of "2 Pilots Destroy Record 23 Tanks" to make the writing more vivid (ten to fifteen minutes). The class reconvenes and a member of each group reads the original passage and the group's rewrite. The class comments on the effects of the original and the rewritten passage.

Purpose: To apply concepts about language to new situations

To improve writing skills

To develop the ability to work productively with others

To develop listening skills

To give respectful feedback to others

Identifying Irony

Description: The class divides into groups who work together to write out Mark Twain's ironic message in *The War-Prayer*. Each group selects a member who pretends to be Twain and reports back to the class what he was saying between the lines.

Purpose: To understand the concept of irony

To develop the skill of drawing reasonable inferences

To develop the ability to work productively with others

To develop listening skills

Shedding Stereotypes

Description: Draw two stick people on the blackboard, one male and the other female. Tell the class that these people are upstanding and active members of their society. Have the class call out sports, jobs, family life, health, and other characteristics for each of these people. Develop these two characters in detail. Then on another part of the board list several stereotype-evoking labels, such as "blind person," "lesbian," and "Mexican." Ask the class to call out stereotypes associated with these labels. Then ask the class two questions. First, is there anything about being blind, a lesbian, or a Mexican that would prevent such a person from being one of the two "upstanding members of society" the class described? Second, is there anything about the stereotypes associated with these labels that would lead people to think they could not be upstanding members of society? Third, ask the class to discuss whether there are stereotypes built into their descriptions of the upstanding members of society they described. Finally, ask the class to recommend what to do to remove negative stereotypes associated with the stereotype-evoking labels. Erase the negative stereotypes from the board and replace them with the new ideas the class has.

Purpose: To develop awareness of stereotypes and how they distort judgments

To develop respect for others

To improve self-esteem

Comparing Exercise Answers

Description: Students form groups to compare and contrast answers to selected exercises (not more than they can do in 10–15 minutes). The teacher moves from group to group checking on their progress and answering questions. The class reconvenes and reports back answers they've found, noting the questions that have "right" answers and the ones that do not.

Purpose: To practice identifying different types of language

To develop the ability to work productively with others

To develop listening skills

QUIZ ITEMS AND ANSWERS

Items

Here are some items to select from when preparing your quizzes.

1. True/False

   a. _____ Ambiguity is generally confusing and should always be avoided.

   b. _____ When we use irony we say the opposite of what we mean to express a more or less subtle criticism.

   c. _____ Weasel words are used by advertisers to make weak claims that look strong.

   d. _____ You can freshen a tired metaphor by extending it.

   e. _____ Unlike weasel words, metaphors are never misleading.

   f. _____ Vivid descriptions evoke precise sensory images; pallid descriptions do not.

   g. _____ General terms are typically pallid but are sometimes necessary in good writing.

   h. _____ To avoid being misled by language, you should become aware of whether a word evokes a positive or negative emotion and ask whether the author has provided evidence relevant to the emotion you experience.

   i. _____ One meaning of the word "he" is "he or she," so using "he" in a paper for "he or she" does not promote stereotypes.

   j. _____ You can shed negative stereotypes by replacing a negative-sounding label with a neutral or more positive-sounding label.

2. For each of the following, discuss whether you find any deliberate ambiguity, irony, misleading weasel words, metaphorical language, vivid or pallid descriptions, or words that evoke or promote stereotypes. Explain your answers in detail.

   a. Am I annoyed that you're late for the third time this week? Of course not; it gives me time to twiddle my thumbs.

   b. A good nurse always treats her patients with respect.

   c. Come on down to Tough Tractors. Our new and improved tractors may last longer than any tractor ever made.

   d. "Eye Deal" as the name of a store that sells glasses

   e. "Battle of the Sexes" used to refer to the relations between men and women

   f. *Rising Tide*, title of a magazine published by the Republican National Committee

   g. "Gutting regulations" used to describe a change in a governmental regulation

   h. I like the way you wash the dishes. The spots you leave create a fascinating design.

   i. You've found a good negotiator when he listens to all the disputing parties.

   j. Employer to female secretaries going out to celebrate their 50th birthdays: "You girls have a good time now."

   k. "Collateral damage" used to describe unintentional injuries to people and property caused by bombs and other weapons during a war

   l. "Sanitary engineer" used to describe a person who cleans toilets

3. Describe possible positive and negative effects of the following types of language.

   a. Ambiguity
   b. Irony
   c. Words like "may," "sometimes," and "seems"
   d. Metaphorical language
   e. Pallid descriptions

Answers

1. True/False

   a. False
   b. True
   c. True
   d. True
   e. False
   f. True
   g. True
   h. True
   i. False
   j. True

2. Identify Ambiguity and Other Devices

   a. This is an example of irony. People don't usually like to be left waiting for three times in a row, and they don't usually describe "twiddling their thumbs" as an activity they want time to do.

   b. Use of "her" here promotes the stereotype that all nurses are female.

   c. The words "new," "improved," and "may" when used with strong-sounding language like "last longer than any tractor ever made" are weasel words.

   d. This is ambiguous when said aloud. When you hear this phrase it sounds like "ideal" or "eye deal." The store's name makes you think you're going to get a good deal on your glasses.

   e. "Battle" is a metaphor here. It implies that the sexes are enemies. It disguises the many common needs and concerns of the sexes, and it disguises the many constructive relations between the sexes.

   f. "Rising Tide" is a metaphor. It compares the Republican party to the incoming tide. I wonder if the person who suggested this metaphor wanted the reader to recognize that tides fall after they rise.

   h. This is an example of irony. People don't usually consider leaving spots on dishes a sign of good dishwashing.

   i. Use of "he" here promotes the stereotype that all negotiators are male.

   j. "Girls" used to describe adult female secretaries promotes the stereotype that female secretaries are not grownups.

   k. "Collateral damage" is a pallid description. It distances the reader from the horrible effects of war on civilians living in a war zone.

   l. "Sanitary engineer" is a positive-sounding label. It implies health, cleanliness, and order. It's also pallid and distances the reader from the activity described. Compare it with "shit scrubber."

3. Describe Positive/Negative Effects

   a. Humorous or intriguing when an audience recognizes the multiple meanings intended; sometimes intentionally or unintentionally misleading.

   b. Can be used to express humor and criticism; sometimes unintentionally confusing when an audience doesn't realize the author means the opposite of what he or she says.

c. These words can be used to let an audience know you are making a weak claim. They become weasel words when they trick an audience into thinking people are making stronger claims than they are.

d. Metaphors sometimes help us see things we didn't see before; sometimes they oversimplify situations they are used to describe. Lively metaphors tend to attract our attention; tired ones tend to go unnoticed.

e. The general terms in pallid descriptions allow us to cover a lot with a few words. They also distance us from the particulars of situations and tend to be somewhat dry and boring compared with vivid descriptions. They're sometimes used to mislead.

CHAPTER 6
SLANTING FOR FUN AND PROFIT

This chapter teaches students the multiple uses of slanting, how to determine the dominant slant of a medium, and how to identify and compensate for potentially misleading slanting in advertising, history reports, news, and information.

SUMMARY

This chapter defines "slanting" as providing a partial and unrepresentative presentation of something. Slanting has a number of effects, including to interest, to inform, to amuse, and to mislead. How we evaluate slanting depends on how we evaluate these effects.

Slanting is different from summarizing, which attempts to produce a brief but representative description of something. Slanting is also different from telling falsehoods, though slanting can be equally misleading.

To determine the dominant slant of a publication or broadcast medium, ask these questions.

1. Who owns the medium?

2. Who provides income to the medium?

3. Who writes and edits for the medium?

4. What audience is the medium directed to?

5. Who supplies information to the medium?

People slant by what they include and omit and by what they highlight and hide. They include or highlight information and points of view that reinforce the impression they are trying to create. They omit or hide information and points of view that are contrary to their desired impression.

Omission occurs within individual reports. It also occurs in the media as a whole when the voices of the powerful are heard significantly more often than the voices of persons from marginalized groups and when stories about significant issues are undercovered.

The following are remedies for slanting by omission.

1. Ask yourself how you would evaluate the situation the story describes and question whether there may be other relevant information that would lead to a different evaluation.

2. Read books, magazines, and newspapers written from perspectives different from those you commonly find in the mass media accounts of history and news.

3. Listen to college radio stations and other alternatives to commercial radio stations.

4. Watch noncommercial television, documentary films, small budget, and international films often shown at universities, colleges, and alternative theaters.

5. Interview people from underrepresented groups about their experiences.

Through language use, placement of information, intensity and size of print, and repetition within a news story in a newspaper or magazine, print media highlight some things and hide others. Because they typically use language that slants; are placed in a prominent position; are printed in large, bold type; and repeat information contained in the story, headlines play an important role in slanting.

Here are some remedies for slanting by highlighting and hiding.

For slanting language, watch for metaphors, words with built-in judgments, and pallid descriptions. Replace with more fitting language words that conceal, sugar coat, distance, or otherwise mislead.

To find slanting by placement, read through the newspaper, looking for short, out-of-the-way articles. Read articles in their entirety, looking carefully for points of view that conflict with points highlighted in the headline and introductory paragraphs. Read the opinion pages and letters to the editor for alternative views.

For slanting by size, intensity, and repetition, question whether the large, bold, or repeated points are the ones you want to remember. Read the article or advertisement in its entirety, looking carefully for points you want to attend to. Reformat the article or advertisement, accentuating the points you want to pay attention to.

For slanted headlines, question whether the headline highlights or hides information you find important in the story. Find information in the story that you would like to highlight. Write your own headline expressing your view of the events the story describes.

People use the same slanting techniques with images, sounds, and smells that they use with printed or spoken information. To counteract slanting with sights and sounds, look and listen carefully to see what emotional impression the sight or sound makes. Question whether the image maker has presented sufficient factual information to support the image's impression. Find information about the event or story you find relevant. Create a sight or sound to illustrate the information.

COMMON PROBLEMS FOR STUDENTS

Students enjoy this chapter and the exercises. However, they have some difficulty with the assignments. When they are asked to write something with a positive or negative slant, they tend to write it as an argument rather than as a report. They have difficulty realizing that you can lead your audience to an evaluation without making evaluative claims. Instead, you quote the evaluative claims of your sources and use other slanting techniques to omit or downplay information that undermines the evaluation you hope to create. Even though some students have difficulty with assignments that ask them to identify and give examples of slanting techniques they and others use, they are often able to improve their papers dramatically after they come to my office and I work through examples with them. Although the material in this chapter seems simple and straightforward, I'd suggest going over lots of examples with students before giving graded assignments.

SAMPLE ANSWERS TO EXERCISES

a. "Our Father in the Vatican"

1. The article, reprinted from *Filipinas*, is directed toward all Filipinos. The content of the article suggests that the audience could be described as primarily Catholic.

2. Positive impression of Jose Cardinal Sanchez

3. The article includes primarily positive information about Father Jose Cardinal Sanchez. The headline "Our Father in the Vatican" uses positive-sounding language, is in bold print, and is placed in a prominent position.

4. "Lost to the Vatican"—this headline emphasizes the information that Father Jose Cardinal Sanchez isn't around much and is little known in the Philippines. It sounds more negative.

b. "Lesbian, Anglican, and Proud."

1. The article, reprinted from *Ms.* magazine, is directed toward feminists. The audience could be described as primarily female, liberal, and of varying sexual orientations.

2. Positive toward the Reverend Roz Hunt

3. She's described in the headline as "Lesbian, Anglican, and Proud." Although to some audiences "lesbian" carries negative associations, it doesn't to a *Ms.* audience. And lesbian, combined with Anglican and proud, suggests something positive. Also, the article starts with "I'm an out dyke," a bold statement made by the Reverend Roz Hunt, which would also please a *Ms.* audience. The information that she must remain celibate to keep her job is put at the end of the article.

4. How about "Hunt Denied Sex by Church"? This puts a more negative spin on the story.

c. "Around the Nation"

1. Yes, conservative Black Americans, or as the magazine describes its audience, "The New Black American Mainstream." You might expect people like Clarence Thomas to read this magazine.

2. At first glance this article looks positive, but it is ironic.

3. The opening phrase, "Coming soon to a campus near you . . ." is well known as a way to build anticipation of a coming event like a new movie or product. Use of this phrase implies all will benefit from "using" the product. This looks positive. However, note the use of the word "victimology." Conservatives use this phrase to suggest that people who aren't in fact victims are trying to make themselves into victims to gain inappropriate sympathy and privileges. Also note that "educate" is in quotations suggesting that these courses aren't really educational.

4. There was no headline on the original article.

d. "Sanctions against Illegal Immigrants"

1. Yes, Hispanics and other immigrants to the United States

2. The article gives a negative impression of H.R. 4.

3. The headline is very telling of the mood of the article; also, Representative Pastor's words, "immigrant bashing . . . ," are slanters, images with built-in judgments. There's no information included about possible positive effects of the legislation.

4. "House Supports Personal Responsibility." This headline creates a positive image of H.R. 4. "Personal Responsibility" sounds good, and for the House to support it sounds positive also.

e. "Black Broadcasters Mad"

1. Yes, Black Americans

2. Negative impression of the FCC decision

3. The title lets the audience know that something's wrong. Only one side of the issue is represented, the African American Broadcasters' point of view. We know nothing of the reaction from the other side except the implied agreement with the legislation.

4. How about "FCC Removes Restrictions"? Because many people don't like restrictions, this could sound good to them.

f. "Truman Doctrine"

1. None is stated by the author, but I'd say it's written for an audience that's complacent about the history of U.S. political and military affairs.

2. This may look neutral because it's fairly bland, especially the heading, but look again at the language used in the article. It puts the Truman Doctrine in a positive light.

3. The title is neutral (unless the reader particularly likes or dislikes Truman). The use of the words "anti-Communist forces" and "to support free people," "armed minorities," and "outside pressures" are emotionally charged phrases intended to slant the reader's opinion in favor of Truman's decision. The author doesn't quote any people who do not support the Truman Doctrine.

4. "Truman Backs Right-Wing Dictator"

g. "The Truman Doctrine"

1. Zinn is writing for "the people." He gives information that is critical of decisions made by leaders.

2. Negative

3. The passage calls the government supported by the Truman Doctrine "a right-wing dictatorship." This puts Truman's doctrine in a negative light. Zinn provides mostly negative information about the doctrine. Although Zinn includes Truman's quote in support of the doctrine, Zinn gives figures for those fighters, supporters, and sympathizers for the "rebellion" that call Truman's quoted claim into question. And Zinn points out that the United States is the main "outside force." Although the United States was acting to "support freedom," the last paragraph of the passage discredits the motivation behind the action by pointing out that although the rebellion was defeated, "illiteracy,

poverty, and starvation remain" along with "a particularly brutal and backward military dictatorship."

    4. "Truman Backs Resistance to Subjugation"

h. Army Ad

    1. This ad is directed toward male high school students who don't have the grades or income to go to college and don't know how they're going to make a living.

    2. A positive impression of life in the army and afterward

    3. "Future" linked with "guarantee" in the headline gives a positive impression. It's soothing to hear these words together if you come from a family that cannot help you get started with an occupation. The bold "Be all that you can be" is hopeful also. The ad includes only the positives about joining the army: delayed entry and training guaranteed in writing up to a year in advance. The images show some of the things you could be doing with your training. What the ad leaves out is the difficulty of breaking your contract if you find that you do have other opportunities or change your mind for other reasons, the presence often of discrimination against gays and lesbians, the hardships that army personnel endure, and the percentage of veterans who are unemployed compared with the general population.

    4. "Guaranteed Loss of Personal Choice"

i. Chevron, "A Tip for Mother Nature"

    1. Environmentally minded gas consumers

    2. Positive

    3. The fish and wildlife pictured are clean and healthy looking. So is the water. No oil slicks or oil-injured birds. The headline, "A Tip for Mother Nature," uses positive-sounding language—"tip" and "Mother Nature"—to make Chevron look good. Words like "flow," "feeds," "nourishes" are all positive-sounding words. The article leaves the impression that the Chevron Corporation does all it can to keep the environment clean, making no mention of the oil refineries it also runs and the drilling efforts maintained to supply them with fossil fuel.

    4. "A Dirty Trick on Mother Nature" with images of oil slicks and damaged birds

j. Jordache, "A Good Pair Makes Great Things Happen"

1. This ad was published in *Seventeen Magazine*, directed toward a young, female audience.

2. Positive

3. The ad uses catchy ambiguity, "A good pair," to refer to the two young women pictured, Chelsi Smith, Miss Universe, and Keylee Sue Sanders, Miss Teen, to the pairing of Jordache with the Starlight Foundation, and, I assume, a good pair of Jordache jeans. The young women have short skirts on in the ads. Does it also refer to a good pair of legs? Did their legs and wearing Jordache clothing enable them to win their titles? Or does the language refer to a good pair of breasts?

    In the small print we find that Jordache Enterprises has made a $40,000 contribution to the Starlight Foundation, which "provides entertainment, educational and wish granting services to critically, chronically and terminally ill children." Although we aren't told what wishes are granted, I just heard that one child wished to go on a bear-killing trip. Apparently the organization planned to grant his wish over the protests of animal rights organizations. I don't know whether he made that wish to Starlight Foundation or some other group, but it does make me wonder about the worth of such organizations.

    I also would like to know more about Jordache. Are their products manufactured in the United States? How much do they pay their workers? Do their workers have health benefits? What's their track record with women and other underrepresented groups?

    Finally, the ad doesn't explain any connection between Jordache or Starlight and the two young women's obtaining their titles.

4. "Pair Feeds Fantasies"

SAMPLE ANSWERS TO READINGS FOR ANALYSIS

Gene Yasuda, "College Students Abusing Plastic"

1. Negative impression of students using credit cards

2. Yes, starting with the headline "College Students Abusing Plastic." The word "abuse" is a negative-sounding word, implying that students cannot use credit wisely. Linking "sex" and "drugs" together in the first sentence also creates a negative impression, as these words combined suggest irresponsibility.

3. Yes, the author starts out with strong negative images of college student credit card use to set his point in the reader's mind. He mentions possible responsible uses

only at the end of the article and in a way that makes credit card companies, not students, look responsible.

4. No students are quoted who talk about their responsible use of credit cards.

5. The first half of the article paints a picture of financially irresponsible students who are unable to resist the temptation of credit. The use of personal experience stories is very powerful in highlighting the author's intended point. The author omits any mention of the responsible use of credit cards. The author also doesn't talk about the broader social and economic context that leads to heavy reliance on credit cards. The author doesn't compare college student "abuse" to "abuse" among the general population. Perhaps it is no worse.

6. "Students Give Credit Its Due" or "Students Learn Credit Responsibility"

"Cuba Accused of Gouging Families of U.S. Exiles to Raise Cash"

1. This story gives a negative impression of Cuba's policies

2. The headline phrase "gouging families" implies that Cuba's tearing holes in families. The article starts out discussing Cuba's ". . . taking advantage of the family ties of U.S. exiles . . ." Also the phrases ". . . a policy of 'extortion'" and "exploiting the love" evoke negative emotional reactions against Cuba. As the mention of the name "Fidel Castro" sets off some people in the United States, using his name in the first sentence will evoke negative emotions in these people, and calling the government Castro's government rather than Cuba's government makes it look like this policy results from Castro's unilateral dictatorial decision. Also "exiles" are people who have been forced to leave their homes. This language creates sympathy for these persons. But it would be interesting to find out who Cubans living in the United States are and why they left Cuba. Were they all forced to leave? If so, why? Did some of them, like many people from Mexico, come here for economic opportunities? Would we call these Mexican people "exiles"? Did some Cubans come here because the Cuban government forced them out? If so, why? Had they been fighting against the Cuban government? What type of government would they like to see in its place?

3. Starting with the headline, the reader is exposed to negative phrasing; this first impression stays in the minds of the readers as they continue the article. Voices calling Cuba's policy into question are placed early in the article. Jorge Ruiz, who questions Mas Canosa's charges, is sandwiched in the middle of the article, and

the U.S. diplomat's statement questioning Mas Canosa's figures comes at the end. Often readers don't read much beyond the headline or first few paragraphs, so using Mas Canosa's voice up front gives a very negative view of Cuba.

4. There are no opinions of Cuban nationals or their families living in the United States, only government officials and politicians.

5. Background information regarding the thirty-year U.S. embargo. I'd like to know more about the economic effects on Cuba of this embargo. I'd also like to know the individual amounts of the taxes on shipping, and other services. Perhaps these amounts aren't individually so high. And if they are high, are they being directed toward people with relatively more income? Are they on items that are "luxuries" rather than "necessities"? Or is Cuba also putting extremely high taxes on food? And I'd like to know what the U.S. government is getting out of the embargo. Is it worth the negative effects of the embargo on the Cuban people? A reading of this story suggests that the United States has imposed an economic embargo that has done nothing for thirty years except cause hardship to the people of Cuba.

6. "US Embargo Proves Taxing for Cuban Expatriates" or "Right-Winger Makes 'Outrageous' Accusations"

Stephen Kinzer, "Managua Rally Cheers Jeane Kirkpatrick"

Answers to questions 1 through 5 were prepared by Julie Thompson.

1. The first three paragraphs (all that many people will read, possibly) place Kirkpatrick and, by extension Reagan and his administration, in the limelight, presenting them as beloved of the Nicaraguan people. But the statement that Kirkpatrick "supports the *violent* overthrow of Nicaragua's Sandinista government" (emphasis mine) clouds this light a bit, as does the Reverend Brockmann's quote: "She is an envoy of death." Kirkpatrick is presented as being strongly allied with the Nicaraguan people, with all her opposition coming from the Nicaraguan government. I believe the result strengthens a black-and-white picture of the Nicaragua situation: in the minds of readers, the people and government are further polarized.

2. Yes. Kinzer used words more to paint a picture than to present facts: "a wildly cheering crowd," "brink of delirium," "filled the air," "fervent reception," "admirers . . . welcoming a film star," and "adulation." The article is written to impress upon the reader that Kirkpatrick is immensely popular with the Nicaraguan people. I think that anyone reading a journalistic source for

information should be wary of adjectives and adverbs: they seem to depend on the writer's subjective judgment and perspective of the event, and it seems there is a danger that such descriptive words have, packaged with them, the author's associative meanings—which may be quite different from the reader's. The language used in the paragraphs offering the position of the Nicaraguan government is also worth mentioning: "The government's response to her speech was, predictably, far different." The word "predictably" functions to neatly categorize and dismiss the government response. In addition, terming Brockmann's response as "lashing out" also rather effectively dismisses him as a man in anger who is thus not to be listened to because he is unreasonable.

3. The headline, lead, and first four paragraphs—the parts that generally determine the direction and force of influence on the reader of the entire article—present only information that supports a favorable view of Kirkpatrick and, by association, the U.S. administration. It is possibly misleading to use the word "rally" in the headline. The group size is stated as "more than 1,000 people," but I suggest that words and phrases positioned in the lead and first two paragraphs give the impression of a larger mass of people—a group representative of the Nicaraguan people as a whole. This implies that "everyone supports and adores Kirkpatrick." Is 1,000 people a large percentage of the Managuan population? Were all 1,000 people Kirkpatrick supporters, or was the group composed partly of police units who were present to monitor and control the crowd? The opinions that represent the other side of the coin are basically limited to two paragraphs farther down in the article than many people will read.

4. I'd like to hear Senator Christopher Dodd's point of view. I'd also like to hear what other countries think of the Contras.

    Nuevo Diario is cited as a "pro-government paper." One would then expect that the paper would present only views that are in accord with or supportive of government philosophy and policy. I would think that the source (the article and the paper) can only be as "expert" as its writers and editors are expert. I do not know whether the paper would deliberately give misinformation, but I would expect that the staff would intelligently and critically evaluate and select which truths/information are to be presented.

    Jose Cruz Garcia is described as a "member of the Conservative party." One would assume that if he had any other credentials to enhance his image as an authority, these would have been stated, but because we are told absolutely nothing else about him, we can only weigh his statement as one man's opinion. It therefore carries very little weight in support of Kirkpatrick's popularity.

Also, as Jose Cruz Garcia is a member of the Conservative party, one would expect him to speak favorably of Kirkpatrick: he gives us no new food for thought.

Reuters: As I know nothing about this news source, I cannot evaluate the information it has furnished.

The Reverend Miguel D'Escoto Brockmann, Nicaraguan foreign minister, is quoted to represent the government response to Kirkpatrick's visit. As a member of the Nicaraguan government, he would be expected to speak against Reagan and Kirkpatrick. I would think that he is in a position to gather relevant information and to judge and comment on that information, but this does not imply that he would have any reason to be objective. The word "expert" doesn't seem to be applicable here. Brockmann may be intelligent, perceptive, and thoroughly knowledgeable about foreign affairs, but, as his views will always represent a particular perspective (one would not expect that he is free to dissent from the government position), can he be an expert? (D. R. replies: Yes. But he is a biased and therefore unreliable expert.)

5. The Kinzer Article could have been improved if it had given more explanation of factors behind the Nicaraguan government's response to Kirkpatrick. Obviously, the Nicaraguan government has complaints against the U.S. government. What are they? Why do the Nicaraguans have these complaints? The article could also have given more details about the military group Kirkpatrick supports that would lead the Reverend Miguel d'Escoto Brockmann to call her an "envoy of death." I'd also like information about how the U.S. government would respond to a foreign diplomat who spoke in support of a military group engaged in an attempt to violently overthrow the U.S. government. Could such a person hope to speak as freely here as Kirkpatrick did in Nicaragua?

6. "Contra Sympathizers Applaud 'Envoy of Death'" or "Nicaragua Goes All Out for Free Speech"

COMMENTS ON WRITING IDEAS

The first four writing ideas ask students to show their understanding of how to apply the slanting techniques described in this chapter. These papers can be graded on the basis of how well students show their understanding of the techniques. You can also require students to use a certain number of techniques and grade in part on whether they used the number required. When assigning the fourth writing idea, remind them that their rewrite should be a news story, not an editorial, and grade them on whether they followed this direction. Their essays can also be graded on the basis of creativity, clarity of writing, and organization.

The fifth writing idea asks students to show their understanding of how to determine the dominant slant of a medium. They'll need to do some research to find the answers to these questions. Their report can be graded on the basis of whether they provided the relevant information and did so with clarity and good organization. The sixth writing idea would make a good freewrite for class discussion when students have finished the chapter assignments.

CLASSROOM ACTIVITIES

Practicing Print Media Slanting

Description: Students work in groups to rewrite the headline and first few paragraphs of a news story to give the story a different slant. The class identifies the effects/purposes and slanting techniques the groups used.

Purpose: To develop the ability to apply slanting techniques to new situations

To develop analytic skills

To improve writing and editing skills

To develop the ability to work productively with others

To learn to distinguish fact from opinion

Giving Voice to Underrepresented Groups

Description: Students role-play characters from different ethnic groups, sexes, ages, countries, income levels, occupations, religions, and political commitments. They all read a mass media news article or one of the above essays for analysis and report back to the class as a whole on whether the article took their perspective into account.

Purpose: To develop the ability to stand in the shoes of others

To become more sensitive to slanting by omission

To develop the ability to work productively with others

To develop respect for others

Identifying Slanting in Visual Media

Description: Students work in groups identifying the effects/purposes and slanting techniques of a short video piece such as a television commercial or an MTV music video.

Purpose: To develop the ability to apply slanting techniques to new situations

To develop analytic skills

To develop the ability to work productively with others

To develop the capacity to think for oneself

Creating a Political Commercial

Description: Students work in groups to create a political commercial to perform for the class. The class identifies the effects/purposes and slanting techniques the groups use.

Purpose: To develop the ability to think creatively

To develop analytic skills

To apply slanting techniques to new situations

To improve speaking and listening skills

To develop the ability to work productively with others

QUIZ ITEMS AND ANSWERS

Items

Here are some items to select from when preparing your quizzes.

  1. True/False

a. _____ According to the text, slanting always has primarily negative effects.

b. _____ Slanting is different from telling falsehoods.

c. _____ According to *Extra!*, there are more conservative than liberal commentators on the weekly current events programs on PBS.

d. _____ Conservatives writing for the *National Review* agree that conservative voices are heard more frequently than liberal ones in the media.

e. _____ Most mass media newspapers are funded primarily by readers.

f. _____ According to Tiffany Devitt, over half the newspaper stories about abortion address how the abortion debate affects politicians.

g. _____ In a study done by Kirk A. Johnson, 85% of the stories about Boston's two mainly black sections reinforced negative stereotypes of blacks.

h. _____ According to the *National Review,* insufficient attention is paid to the resentments of the underclass.

i. _____ One way to learn to recognize slanting by omission is to read books, magazines, and newspapers written from perspectives different from those you commonly find in the mass media's accounts of history and news.

j. _____ Headlines are a slanter's delight because they provide the opportunity to make use of a full range of slanting techniques.

2. Short Answer

   a. How does the text define "slanting"?

   b. How does the text define "summarizing"?

   c. List a positive and a negative effect of slanting.

   d. The text lists five questions to ask to determine the dominant slant of a medium. What are three of them?

   e. Suppose a liberal reporter covers a political story. Would that reporter's published story have a liberal slant? Explain.

   f. What did the label "Desert Storm" highlight or hide about the 1990 U.S. military action in the Persian Gulf?

   g. According to the text, where do news people place stories and information they want to highlight?

3. The text names three persons or groups whose reputation has been affected by omission: Christopher Columbus, Native American Women, and Martin Luther King. Select one of them. Describe the omitted information and the change in reputation created by including this information.

4. Write a headline for the following that fits what you know to be true about the story or product but creates a very different impression from the existing headline.

(Insert an ad or news story you've found or one from the exercises at the end of the chapter that you didn't discuss in class.)

Answers

1. True/False

   a. False
   b. True
   c. True
   d. False
   e. False
   f. False
   g. True
   h. False
   i. True
   j. True

2. Short Answer

   a. Slanting is providing a partial and unrepresentative presentation of a particular position, opinion, or phenomenon.

   b. Summarizing is producing a brief but representative presentation of something.

   c. Positive effects include creating interest, amusing an audience, and informing an audience. The main negative effect is misleading an audience.

   d. The five questions are these: Who owns the medium? Who provides income to the news medium? Who writes and edits for the news medium? What audience is the medium directed toward? Who supplies information to the news medium?

   e. Not necessarily. It depends on who edits the story and what sources the reporter uses. A conservative editor has the opportunity to slant the story, and the reporter may not create a liberal slant in the first place if doing so would offend sources the reporter hopes to use in the future.

    f. "Desert Storm" hid the image of people being killed by modern weapons. It also made the military action and its effects seem like an act of nature instead of something that humans are responsible for.

    g. Place a story you want to highlight on the front page; place information you want to highlight in the headline and first part of the story.

3. Affected by Omission

Christopher Columbus. The information that's omitted describes the details of Columbus's involvement in enslaving the Indians of Hispaniola. This information contributes to a negative impression of Columbus.

Native American Women. The information that's typically omitted describes the ways Native American women resisted oppression and cultural assimilation. This information contributes to the impression that these women are not passive, but active in protecting their culture.

Martin Luther King. The information that's typically omitted is King's concern with the "glaring contrast of poverty and wealth." This information contributes to an impression of King as more politically radical than is commonly thought.

4. Write Headline

Any headline that highlights truths about the product or story and creates a very different impression from the original title

CHAPTER 7
EVALUATING ARGUMENTS: AN OVERVIEW

This chapter provides an overview of the basic concepts of argument evaluation: acceptable support, relevant support, and sufficient support. It teaches students ways to arrive at acceptable support, the importance of background knowledge for identifying relevant support and counterconsiderations, how to distinguish inductive sufficiency from deductive validity, and methods for establishing deductive invalidity.

SUMMARY

For support to establish an acceptable conclusion, the support itself must be acceptable. The standard ways of arriving at acceptable support include personal experience, ecstatic experience, self-evident truths, inferential knowledge, authority, and common knowledge. Personal experience includes sensory experience obtained through the five senses and awareness of our internal experiences. To determine whether to accept a claim on the basis of personal experience, ask these questions.

> Is there any reason to think the witnesses' personal experiences do not give a full or accurate account of what happened?

> Is there any reason to think the witnesses misremember, are not fully candid about, or make claims that go beyond their personal experience?

> Is there any reason to think you might not fully understand what the witness was saying?

Ecstatic experience is the sense of losing oneself as an individual, of being connected with everything. Some people believe that ecstatic experience gives humans knowledge of divinity; others do not.

Self-evident truths are statements that we know to be true without personal experience or argument. Once you know the meaning of the terms in a self-evident claim, you recognize that the claim has to be true; it's impossible for something to be a circle and a square. Many people also believe that basic moral principles are self-evident.

Inferential knowledge is the conclusion of a strong argument. Because not all our inferences are based on strong arguments, we must check the strength of the support on which those inferences are based to determine whether they in fact yield knowledge. Ask the following questions.

Is the support acceptable?

Is the support relevant to its conclusion?

Is the support sufficient to establish its conclusion?

Expertise is relatively advanced knowledge of a field or subject. To question whether to base support on a claim of expertise, ask these questions.

Is the authority's degree of expertise sufficient for your purposes?

Is the authority's scope of expertise sufficient for your purposes?

Is the authority's claim controversial?

Is there any reason to think the authority might not be fully candid?

Are you being unduly influenced by the person's looks or how the person talks?

Is there any reason to think you might not fully understand the authority's report?

If you're trying to decide whether to follow an authority's command, ask these questions.

Does the person have the right to make commands?

Is the command within the scope of the person's authority?

Common knowledge is settled, uncontroversial belief for which support could be provided, if necessary. Here are some questions to ask to determine whether a claim is common knowledge or shared ignorance.

Is there general agreement—beyond your usual circle of acquaintances—about this claim?

Is the claim acceptable on the basis of personal experience, ecstatic experience, self-evident truth, inferential knowledge, or reliable authority?

Relevant support provides some reason to accept its conclusion. A relevant counterconsideration provides some reason to reject a conclusion. As a rule, we identify supports and counterconsiderations *as* supports and counterconsiderations because we believe they have an evidential link to a conclusion. However, people sometimes offer supports and counterconsiderations that have no evidential link to a conclusion. And other times, the evidential link is not clear to an audience because the audience does not have enough background knowledge to see the link.

The straw person fallacy is one common way that argument makers provide irrelevant counterconsiderations. People commit the straw person fallacy when they misrepresent a position, making the position appear weaker than it is. To avoid the straw person fallacy, use the principle of charity. Be generous when trying to understand the claims of others, especially those claims you expect to disagree with.

Ignorance of an audience's needs, goals, and values provides an opportunity to offer irrelevant support. We also sometimes provide irrelevant support when we have false background beliefs about how things are connected in the world, such as the connection between the inability to speak a language and the ability to understand what one sees. Here are some questions to ask when checking support for relevance:

> Has the author blown down a straw position or provided support that's irrelevant to the audience's needs, goals, or values?

> Did the author have a false background belief, one that linked things that aren't linked?

> Do you have enough background information about the author and the subject to figure out the author's intentions and to see the evidential link between the support and the conclusion?

Sufficient support establishes the acceptability of the conclusion (assuming the support is also acceptable). Whether support is sufficient depends, in part, on how the conclusion is stated. Strongly stated conclusions, which use words like "very likely," require more support than more weakly stated conclusions, which use words like "possibly."

There are no rules for determining sufficiency that can be applied to every argument, but we can get a sense of how to achieve sufficiency by looking at some common types of arguments. In the *argument from analogy*, we assert that because something is true of one thing, it is true of something else. We justify our inference by saying the two things are analogous, and describe similarities between the two things. The stronger the similarities and weaker the dissimilarities between the two things being compared, the more sufficient is the inference.

In *generalizing from a sample*, we assert that because something is true of a sample (a part), it is true of the whole group. We justify our inference by providing evidence that the sample is similar to, representative of, the whole. The more things you do to ensure that your sample is representative, the stronger is the inference from the sample.

When *reasoning to an explanation*, we attempt to rule out alternative explanations. The more alternative explanations the support rules out, the more sufficient is the support. False fault finding—thinking we are wholly responsible for something we are at most only marginally responsible for—is one way to fail to provide sufficient support for an explanation.

Emotion-evoking support is necessary for supporting some claims, like "Let's get out of here" (Support: There's a fire in the house). But sometimes people act from impulse without thinking a decision through. When using emotion-evoking support (support that produces an emotional response) be sure to keep in mind the following questions.

Is the emotion-evoking support relevant to the conclusion?

Is the emotion-evoking support intense enough to be distracting?

Is the emotion-evoking support supplemented with additional support needed to rule out alternative ways to serve the goals, needs, and values relevant to the problem?

Some general guidelines for improving the fit between an argument's conclusion and supports are these:

Add additional support and rule out counterconsiderations.

Weaken a conclusion you don't have sufficient support to hold up. Replace "definitely" with "very likely" or "possibly."

Strengthen a conclusion for which you have more than enough support. Replace "possibly" with "very likely" or "definitely."

In a *deductive argument* we claim that the conclusion follows with necessity from the support. (Arguments that make weaker claims about the relation between conclusion and support are called "inductive.")

Rules with no exceptions or with very explicitly defined exceptions provide an opportunity to reason deductively. People also reason deductively when they are reasoning from the rules of mathematics.

An argument with deductively sufficient support is called "valid." When a deductive argument is valid, it's *impossible* for the support to be acceptable and the conclusion unacceptable. A deductive argument whose support does not necessitate its conclusion is called "invalid." A valid argument with acceptable support is called "sound." A deductive argument with at least one unacceptable support is called "unsound."

To identify an argument as invalid try one of the following:

Check to see whether the deductive argument has true support and a false conclusion. If it does, it cannot be valid.

Fill in the story. For deductive arguments written in general terms, try to fill in the story in a way to make the supports true and the conclusion false. If you can, the argument is invalid.

Think up a refuting analogy: an argument with the same structure as the argument whose validity you question and which has true support and a false conclusion. Because the refuting argument is invalid, the argument you are questioning is also invalid.

COMMON PROBLEMS FOR STUDENTS

There's a lot of material in this chapter. Take it easy. I spend a week on the section on acceptability and review points again and again during the rest of the semester. I focus on questioning authorities as much of student writing is based on authority. The points and questions seem obvious, but putting them into action is another thing. Students are used to quoting without question anything they find in print. They are puzzled about how to get information about the authors of articles and books they read to determine whether they are worth quoting, so plan to give them some ideas about how to do that.

There's much philosophical controversy about ecstatic experience and self-evident knowledge. Because I teach an introductory class in critical thinking, I don't get into these controversies in detail, but students enjoy some discussion of these heady topics. It gives them a break from the more mundane inquiry about how to find an authority's credentials.

As for the overview on relevance and sufficiency, I treat this as an overview and don't spend much time on it. I think students get a better understanding of how to evaluate arguments by looking at types of arguments in more detail (the topics of the next three chapters).

I keep the discussion of deductive arguments short, because I don't find detailed discussions of deductive logic particularly useful for sorting through information and arguments in everyday life. Nonetheless, in my classes, I supplement the text with a brief discussion of the syllogism and simple examples of symbolizing arguments.

Students seem to enjoy learning about validity because it's so weird that an argument can be valid and yet have absurd premises. They have trouble recognizing invalid arguments that have true conclusions. They also get confused about using the word "validity" the way logicians use it because in common parlance, "validity" is used for acceptability or truth.

SAMPLE ANSWERS TO EXERCISES

1. a. *Conclusion:* "So either God isn't totally good, or God doesn't cause everything."

Support 1: "Millions of people and animals have suffered and died from earthquakes, famines and disease." Acceptable on the basis of common knowledge. Also, read the paper, listen to the news; basic library research will confirm that this claim is acceptable.

Support 2: "When you suffer or die you are harmed." Acceptable. Acceptable by definition.

Support 3: "Being harmed is evil." Depends on how you define "evil." If evil is defined as intentional harm, then the claim is unacceptable. If it's any harm, then the claim is acceptable by definition.

Support 4: "It's not possible to be totally good and cause evil." Once again, this depends on what's meant by "being totally good." If being totally good means that one never causes intentional or unintentional harm, then it's true by definition. If not, then it's questionable. One can be a good person and still sometimes do intentional or unintentional harm.

b. *Conclusion:* "No one can know that gods or goddesses exist."

Support 1: "The only way to know that something exists is by using your senses. You have to see, hear, taste, touch, or smell something to know it exists." Questionable. We cannot see, hear, taste, touch, or smell emotions, either; yet they exist; we feel them in a different way.

Support 2: "No one can see, hear, touch, taste, or smell gods and goddesses." Acceptable on the basis of common knowledge, unless, like Christ, the gods or goddesses are in human form.

c. *Conclusion:* "You should believe that a god or goddess exists."

Support 1: "The world looks and feels different to someone who believes in the supernatural. It's a richer, more mysterious place." Unacceptable, if you take the claim as a generalization, because people will vary. Some could find the world a richer, more mysterious place. Others could find it frightening and confusing.

Support 2: "Also, you'll want to please the god or goddess. As a result, you'll be more likely to treat others well if you believe a god or goddess exists." Questionable. That you will be more likely to treat others well is a subconclusion, and the fact that one wants to please the god or goddess isn't sufficient support to back it up. You need to know that the god or goddess values treating others well. Assuming this is true, then you also have to determine whether those who believe in a god or goddess do try to please the god or goddess. You also have to determine whether the believer will do what the believer wants to do. If so and if the god or goddess values treating others well, then the subconclusion is acceptable.

d. *Conclusion:* "People who believe in a male god should add a female god to their worship."

Support 1: "A male god gives men the hope that they can improve themselves spiritually, but does little for women." *Subsupport:* "For women could not be formed in a male god's image." Questionable. The subsupport is insufficient. It implies that role models do not cross gender lines. Dr. Martin Luther King was a role model to men and women alike in pursuing racial equality. Rosa Parks inspired both men and women to boycott the bus service when she refused to move to the back of the bus.

Support 2: "[Men and women] should worship male and female gods." *Subsupport:* "Men and women should respect each other as equally godlike." The subsupport is acceptable; it implies understanding that all genders are equal and therefore worthy of respect as role models. However, it doesn't follow that men and women should worship male and female gods. First, the argument maker must establish that it's not possible to recognize the equality of men and women without worshipping male and female gods.

e. *Conclusion:* "I cannot myself feel that . . . in the matter of virtue Christ stands quite as high as some other people (Buddha and Socrates) known in history."

Support 1: "There is one serious defect in my mind in Christ's moral character, and that is that he believed in hell. I do not myself feel that any person who is really profoundly humane can believe in everlasting punishment." Questionable. Russell needs to explain why a person cannot be profoundly humane and believe in everlasting punishment. Russell also claims that Christ is vindictive and that being vindictive distracts from excellence. The claim that being vindictive distracts from excellence is common knowledge.

Subsupport: "Christ certainly as depicted in the Gospels did believe in everlasting punishment, and one does find repeatedly a vindictive fury against those people who would listen to His preaching." Acceptable, assuming you accept the Bible as authoritative. The biblical reference is accurate; Christ did believe in everlasting punishment, and he did express a fury when not heeded, especially in the marketplace in the temple which he perceived as blasphemous.

Subsupport: "You will find in the Gospels Christ said, 'Ye serpents, ye generation of vipers, how can ye escape the damnation of hell?' That was said to people who did not like His preaching." Acceptable. These words are a direct quote from the Bible, the book of authority on Christ.

Support 2: "You do not, for instance, find that attitude in Socrates. You find him quite bland and urbane toward people who would not listen to him." Assuming Plato's description of Socrates is accurate, Socrates was not vindictive, even when sentenced to death for questioning. (However, Socrates had other traits that aren't entirely laudatory, including mocking people who were less adept at reasoning than he was. He comes across as quite arrogant at times.)

f. *Conclusion:* "Man is a sociable being, and it is for aught I know one of the worst of punishments to be excluded from society."

Support 1: The entire story regarding the prisoner in the Bastille. Whether this is acceptable or not depends on whether the person who told it to Franklin is a reliable witness. However, one can easily imagine that such a situation would be very unpleasant.

Support 2: "One of the philosophers, I think it was Plato, used to say that he had rather be the veriest stupid block in nature, than the possessor of all knowledge without some intelligent being to communicate it to." Potentially acceptable. Because Mr. Franklin is unsure of his citation, it is difficult to accept this support as strong.

2. a. *Conclusion:* "You should believe that a god or goddess exists."

Support 1: "The world looks and feels different (richer and more mysterious) to someone who believes in the supernatural." Relevant. Enhanced quality of life gives some reason for belief.

Support 2: "You'll be more likely to treat others well if you believe a god or goddess exists." Relevant. Improved behavior gives some reason to adopt a belief.

b. *Conclusion:* "People who believe in a male god should add a female god to their worship."

Support 1: "A male god gives men the hope that they can improve themselves spiritually, but does little for women." Relevant. The inadequacy of a male god gives some reason to add a female god.

Support 2: "Men and women should worship male and female gods." Relevant. That men and women should worship male and female gods implies that they should add a female god to their worship, if they don't have one already.

c. *Conclusion:* "I cannot myself feel that . . . in the matter of virtue Christ stands quite as high as some other people (Buddha and Socrates) known in history."

Support 1: Christ believed in hell and was vindictive. Relevant. The issue at hand is Christ's humanity, by showing that Christ was supportive of "everlasting punishment," the author attempts to paint a picture of an inhumane Christ.

Support 2: Socrates was urbane, not vindictive. Relevant. This helps establish that Christ has less moral excellence than Socrates.

d. *Conclusion 1:* Implied—"Dad, I would like you to send me some extra money this month."

Support: "No, I've just had some unexpected expenses, and I'm short." Relevant, as it confirms he is short of cash.

Conclusion 2: "I'm sorry, son." Implied no.

Support: "Our agreement was that if I paid for your tuition, books, and rent you would work and pay for the rest from your part-time job." Relevant in that it reiterates the agreement the conclusion is based on.

Conclusion 3: Impress your friend with your sense of humor.

Support: "That's how I impressed your mom." How relevant this is depends on how much the son's and the father's situations are like each other.

e. *Conclusion:* "The tenure system should be abolished."

1. *Support:* "It's virtually impossible to get fired with tenure, regardless of poor productivity." Relevant in that it states a reason that tenure is not a good idea.

2. *Support:* "College professors should be judged by productivity, just like everyone else." Relevant. It gives a reason that tenure (which operates independent from productivity) should be abolished.

f. *Conclusion:* "The tenure system should continue."

1. *Support:* "Professors will be more likely to teach unpopular views if they do not fear getting fired." Relevant. This gives a reason to accept the tenure system.

2. *Support:* "Unpopular views should be taught." Relevant. This gives a reason to accept the tenure system.

g. *Conclusion:* "Counties should pass domestic partnership laws allowing unmarried persons who live together to share health insurance and other benefits, the way married couples do."

1. Support: "After all, lesbian and gay couples need health insurance and other benefits as much as heterosexual couples do." Relevant. Need for health insurance is a reason for making it easier for persons to get health insurance.

2. Support: "It's unfair to exclude homosexuals and lesbians from receiving social goods." Relevant. Increasing fairness is a reason for modifying laws.

h. *Conclusion:* "So we should go ahead and get married."

1. Support: "But we both have jobs, and we love each other." Relevant, as it lists valid and pertinent reasons to get married.

2. Support: "Besides, our parents would like us to get married." Relevant. This shows there's some social support that could help make the marriage work.

i. *Conclusion:* "You should come to class whether or not you've finished the paper due that day."

Support: "Otherwise, you commit two sins: missing class and not having your paper in on time." Relevant. If missing class is wrong, then that evaluation provides some reason that one should go to class.

j. *Conclusion:* "You should let me turn in my paper late."

Support: "I've had to stay up all night with a sick child, and I haven't been able to think well enough to write." Whether this is relevant depends on the criteria the teacher (and class) established for permitted late papers. If the class is on procrastination, the teacher may not accept the excuse as a good one. The student should not have waited until the last minute to finish the paper.

k. *Conclusion:* "To take it a step further, I am asking you to consider not selling them (ornate box turtles) either."

1. Support: "The book stated that even experienced reptile handlers have difficulty keeping ornate box turtles alive for any length of time." Relevant to a shop owner who cares about the quality and length of life of pets sold. Factual information from a reliable source that discusses the difficulties of keeping the animals alive in captivity.

2. Support: "We all suffered grief while watching our little turtle refuse food, refuse to stay awake in spite of our efforts with a bath every morning, respond to warmth, love, tidbits, attention, no attention, prayers. Still, she died one day." Relevant to a shop owner who cares about the feelings of customers.

Support: "Human habitat is not conducive to any kind of longevity for many of the 'pets' sold in pet stores, and the article urged the reader not to buy these threatened animals as pets." Relevant to a shop owner who cares about the quality and length of life of pets.

3. a. *Inductive.* "Unlikely" modifies the conclusion.

   b. *Deductive.* Though the conclusion isn't asserted to follow with necessity, it does. It follows from the claims made in the support.

   c. *Inductive.* This argument relies on a comparison of Dad's experience with his son's; an argument maker wouldn't state that its conclusion follows with necessity.

   d. *Deductive.* Though the conclusion isn't asserted to follow with necessity, it does. The conclusion follows from a definition.

   e. *Inductive.* The author puts a "probably" in the conclusion.

   f. *Inductive.* The conclusion isn't asserted to follow with necessity. And the supports as stated don't imply that the conclusion must be true. Perhaps the car has snow tires. Maybe the passengers are risk takers.

   g. *Deductive.* Though the conclusion isn't asserted to follow with necessity, the conclusion that a first cause exists does follow with necessity. (That the first cause is God, however, needs additional support).

4. a. *Conclusion:* "You've got to fight and get away from Albert."

   Main support: "He ain't no good." Nettie provides ample evidence that Albert is unworthy of her affection. However, Celie may have to work out some practical details before she can follow Nettie's advice. Celie may not know how to get away or where to go.

   b. *Conclusion:* "Choose your new family member from one of the 70,000 unplanned puppies or kittens born every day," and at least don't buy a purebred for its looks only.

   Support: Nearly all the dogs I've euthanized based on temperament were purebreds.

   Support: Purebreds are medical nightmares.

   Implied counterconsideration: Purebreds look good and are in fashion.

Response: Looks and fashion are all right for shoes, but not for dogs. Behavior is more important.

The author gives strong reasons not to buy a purebred for its looks only, though his reasons may not satisfy someone who cares more about showing an animal than about the quality of that animal's life and the people it comes into contact with. The author also provides evidence that purebreds he knows have more problems than other dogs, but whether this evidence is sufficient depends on whether his experience with purebreds is representative.

5. a. *Invalid.* It is possible that the ice cream could melt even if the refrigerator were not unplugged. The temperature control could be set too low; the ice cream could be left on the counter.

   b. *Valid.* This argument is based on a definition, and by definition unacceptable support yields a weak argument.

   c. *Invalid.* One of the options was both, so her being in the kitchen does not necessarily mean she was not in the living room.

   d. *Invalid.* There are other reasons a car could overheat. Perhaps the thermostat is broken or the radiator is dry.

   e. *Invalid.* The possibility that Mario is playing the fiddle in the living room was not disproved, so we do not know yet whether he is home.

   f. *Invalid.* The computer might be on a three-foot-tall table next to the desk.

6. a. If no computer functions when it's not plugged in, then my IBM laptop doesn't function when it's not plugged in.

   But my laptop computer is capable of running on battery power without being plugged in.

   Therefore, not all computers must be plugged in to function.

   b. If smoking always causes lung cancer, then George Burns who smoked all his life would develop lung cancer.

   George Burns died of old age this year and did not have lung cancer.

   Therefore, smoking does not always cause lung cancer.

   c. If all advertisements evoke emotions, then this ad showing the new location of JP's Grill evokes emotion.

But this ad showing the new location of JP's Grill doesn't evoke emotions.

Therefore, it's false that all advertisements evoke emotions.

d. If every married physicist has a wife, then no married women are physicists.

But some married women are physicists.

Therefore, it's false that every married physicist has a wife.

e. If all women want to be mothers, then Carla wants to be a mother.

But Carla does not want to have children.

Therefore, not all women want to be mothers.

f. If it's always wrong to break a promise, then it's wrong for John to break his promise to wash Karen's car after school, even though he broke his ankle and was hospitalized.

But it's not wrong for John to break his promise to Karen under these conditions.

So it's not always wrong to break a promise.

g. If you should never do anything to cause another person pain, then the doctor should not give me a painful tetanus shot when I step on a rusty nail.

But it is acceptable for a doctor to give me a painful tetanus shot.

Therefore, it's not always wrong to cause another person pain.

h. If all arguments from analogy are inductive arguments, the analogies used to show weakness in the structure of deductive arguments are inductive.

But analogies used to show the weakness in the structure of deductive arguments are not inductive.

Therefore, not all arguments from analogy are inductive arguments.

SAMPLE ANSWERS TO READINGS FOR ANALYSIS

Robert Coles, "Drugs Should Not Be Legalized"

1. He quotes an unnamed law professor and a mother of four children. Legalizing drugs will cut down on drug crime, though maybe not as quickly as the quotation implies. Also, I have no reason to doubt that the mother of four felt uncared for by

the professor she heard. She may have misinterpreted his intent, however. Coles apparently finds the claims acceptable.

2. No. The professor is discussing the issue of social violence and illegal drug sales, not the topic of drug abuse among users.

3. Yes. He implies that those who support the legalization of drugs have no understanding or concern about whether people are addicted to them. In fact, those who support legalization often address the issue of drug addiction. They just don't find criminalizing drugs the best way to respond to the problem.

4. Yes, the mother's response is emotion evoking. It is relevant to consider the possibility that legalizing drugs reinforces drug use. It is not sufficient, however, as there may be other, better ways to respond to drug addiction.

5. Keeping drugs illegal will not solve her problem. This is evident because drugs are illegal now and the problem exists. Coles's solution is a "social order that responds to and clearly evokes a firm moral tradition." There is no convincing support presented for this solution.

Eric Scigliano, "Drugs Should Be Legalized"

1. Yes, by referring to the decrease in alcohol and tobacco as a result of "sending the right message"; he uses that situation as an explanation for how the legalization of drugs can decrease drug use if combined with "sending the right message."

2. Yes. He claims that legalizing drugs is like legalizing alcohol at the end of prohibition.

3. Yes, he talks of restrictions on the sale of recreational drugs. He also talks of the benefits to inner-city kids of silencing the message that drugs equal wealth and power. And he recognizes that the underlying problems for kids living in the ghetto, such as unemployment and racism, need to be addressed.

4. His conclusion is stated in very general terms; his argument would be stronger if he elaborated on it. What drugs is he talking about legalizing? All street drugs? But he does a good job of responding to some of the main counterconsiderations against legalizing drugs.

5. No right answer.

Donald Kagan, "Military Service: A Moral Obligation"

1. "When a citizen has become an adult and has not chosen to leave the country, he tacitly approves of its legitimacy and consents to its laws. He benefits from their protection and has the moral obligation to obey them if he wants to stay."

2. Yes, it is valid. That is, if the premises are true, the conclusion must be true.

3. No, it's false that citizens' refusal to serve in a war they disapprove of destroys a democracy. People refused to serve in Vietnam without destroying the U.S. democracy. The argument is unsound.

4. It's a bit confusing. He seems to be saying that citizens have a duty to accept all decisions by legitimate governments (even ones that go against their consciences) and that a decent, free society won't expect them to act on that duty (in cases when it goes against their consciences). But if they have a duty not to refuse to fight, then why is it right to allow them to refuse?

Emily S. Guttchen, "Rebuttal to 'Military Service: A Moral Obligation'"

1. No, she picks certain aspects of his argument to focus on offering a distorted view of some of his ideals.

2. No. It assumes consistency in the parts based on the whole. For example, just because the whole car is heavy doesn't mean all its parts are heavy.

3. No. His criterion for a "legitimate state" is "one that permits the open advocacy of different opinions, the possibility of changing the laws by peaceful means and, most important, emigration without penalty." Presumably decisions made by legitimate states are legitimate. In any case, he expects citizens to accept decisions made by "duly elected and appointed bodies and officials," even if they are wrong.

4. Family, culture, and home

5. No. She feels the focus should be placed more on stopping wars before they start and removing threats of nuclear war.

6. No right answer

COMMENTS ON WRITING IDEAS

The first two writing ideas are probably the most difficult for students because they aren't used to evaluating their own arguments. They assume that by writing them they've already determined that the arguments are strong. It's a jarring experience for students to reflect consciously on the strength of their arguments. Have them evaluate an argument they've written, if only as an ungraded assignment for class discussion. The second assignment is a great way to get some tips about good teaching—and to find out that students care about learning. I've found they really pour their hearts into this assignment.

The third writing idea asks students to evaluate someone else's argument. Assigning the fourth writing idea will help you find confusions and insights that your students have about the distinction between induction and deduction. The fifth and sixth writing ideas give students an opportunity to express their own ideas about the subjects of this chapter.

CLASSROOM ACTIVITIES

Argument Evaluation Clinic

Description: Students form groups of "experts" specializing in different aspects of argument evaluation. They use their expertise on one of the essays for analysis, then report their findings and recommendations back to the class. Before they form into groups, however, the class as a whole breaks the argument into its parts, identifying the main conclusions and main supports and removing support avoidance and support enhancers. The experts include the following:

Acceptability Accountants: (1) Determine whether the main support statements are acceptable. (2) Offer information to help explain the acceptability of any questionable statement or provide other acceptable support relevant to the essay's conclusion.

Righteous Relevance Relators: (1) Determine whether the main support statements are relevant to the conclusion. (2) Provide background information that helps show how the support helps establish the conclusion.

| Sufficiency Superiors | (1) Imagine possibilities (alternative policies or explanations to the one the conclusion provides) that the support does not rule out. (2) Determine whether the possibilities are likely enough to undermine accepting the conclusion (keeping in mind how firmly the conclusion is stated). |
| Language Lovers | (1) Find examples of words that need to be defined to be understood. (2) Offer definitions for the words. |

Purpose: To develop the ability to apply concepts of argument evaluation

To develop analytic ability

To develop the ability to work productively with others

To develop the capacity to think for oneself

Evaluating Argument in the Context of Conflict

Description: Students divide into groups and select a decision they disagree about. They listen to and write down each other's reasons. They then evaluate each other's reasons. When they have finished, they discuss their evaluations with each other and report back to the class.

Purpose: To develop the ability to apply the concepts of argument evaluation

To develop respect for others

To develop the capacity to think for oneself

To develop the ability to resolve conflicts

Questioning Authorities

Description: The class divides into groups and develops scenarios in which someone (student, worker, child) refuses to act on an inappropriate command made by an authority (teacher, boss, parent). The groups perform their scenarios for the class.

Purpose: To develop the ability to distinguish appropriate from inappropriate commands

To cultivate emotional health and well-being

To cultivate integrity

To develop the ability to act in accord with one's values

Courting Confusion

Description: Students do 10-minute looping freewrites in which they start with the phrase "When it comes to argument evaluation, I'm confused about . . ." They write for a few minutes then repeat (loop back to) the opening phrase and write some more. They continue freewriting then loop back again to the opening phrase and keep going. Afterward, they report their confusions, and the teacher facilitates a discussion about how to sort through the confusions they found.

Purpose: To become aware of confusion

To use confusion to reach a deeper understanding of argument evaluation

To develop the ability to think creatively

To develop the capacity to think for oneself

QUIZ ITEMS AND ANSWERS

1. True/False

   a. Personal experience includes the kinesthetic sense as well as the senses of touch, taste, sight, hearing, and smell.

   b. Reports of personal experience are always acceptable.

   c. Some people base belief in God on ecstatic experience.

   d. The following claim is self-evident: "Grass is green."

   e. The conclusions of strong subarguments are examples of inferential knowledge.

   f. Sometimes people believe what an expert says because of how the expert looks.

g. According to Stanley Milgram's research, people are unlikely to follow inappropriate commands.

h. People sometimes mistake mere assumption or shared ignorance for common knowledge.

i. When you are determining relevance in an inductive argument, it doesn't matter whether you know a lot or a little about the topic of the argument.

j. The principle of charity states that teachers should bring treats to class at least once a semester.

k. Sometimes people confuse political satire with straw person reasoning.

l. Whether support is sufficient or not depends on how strongly the conclusion is stated.

2. The text lists six questions to ask when you are determining the reliability of an expert. What are four of them?

3. Define the following terms:

a. Sufficient support

b. Valid argument

c. Sound argument

4. What are some principal contrasts between inductive and deductive arguments?

5. Underline the conclusions of the following arguments. Are the arguments valid or invalid? If you find an argument invalid, provide a refuting analogy. If you believe the argument is valid, explain why.

a. All fish swim.
All trout swim.
Therefore, all trout are fish.

b. All dogs bark.
All cats meow.
So, cats are not dogs.

c. All dogs bark.
No cats bark.
Thus, cats are not dogs.

d. President Clinton is the chair of the philosophy department at [your university].
All chairs of philosophy departments are philosophers.
Therefore President Clinton is a philosopher.

    e. All beagles bark.
       Some dogs bark.
       So, some dogs are beagles.

    f. If all paper is white, then yellow paper is white. But yellow paper is not white, so it's false that all paper is white.

    g. The telephone book advertising pages are not white. Here's why. If the telephone book advertising pages are not white, then it's false that all paper is white.

6. Are the arguments under (5) sound? Explain.

Answers

1. True/False

    a. True
    b. False
    c. True
    d. False
    e. True
    f. True
    g. False
    h. True
    i. False
    j. False
    k. True
    l. True

2. Four of the following:

Is the expert's degree of expertise sufficient for your purposes?

Is the expert's scope of expertise sufficient for your purposes?

Is the expert's claim controversial?

Is there any reason to think the expert might not be fully candid?

Are you paying attention to how the expert looks rather than to whether the expert is reliable?

Is there any reason to think you might not fully understand the expert's report?

3. a. Sufficient support establishes the acceptability of the conclusion (provided that the support is itself acceptable).

   b. In a valid argument, it's impossible for the supports to be true and the conclusion false.

   c. A sound argument is valid and has acceptable supports.

4. An inductive argument's conclusion is not asserted to follow with necessity from its supports. The conclusion of a strong inductive argument adds information not contained in the supports. Inductive sufficiency admits of degrees. Adding additional support and ruling out counterpossibilities increases the sufficiency of inductive support.

   A deductive argument's conclusion is asserted to follow with necessity from its supports. In a valid deductive argument, the conclusion is already contained in the supports. Deductive sufficiency does not admit of degrees; a deductive argument is either valid or invalid.

5. a. *Conclusion:* All trout are fish.

      Invalid

      Refuting analogy:

      All doctors went to college.

      All lawyers went to college.

      All lawyers are doctors.

   b. *Conclusion:* Cats are not dogs.

      Invalid

      Refuting analogy:

      All fish swim.

      All trout breath through gills.

      Trout are not fish.

   c. *Conclusion:* Cats are not dogs.

      Valid. Since all dogs bark, anything that does not bark cannot be a dog.

      Cats don't bark, so cats cannot be dogs.

d. *Conclusion:* President Clinton is a philosopher.

Valid: Since all philosophy department chairs are philosophers, anyone who is a philosophy department chair is a philosopher. If President Clinton were a philosophy department chair, he would be a philosopher.

e. *Conclusion:* Some dogs are beagles.

Invalid

Refuting analogy:

All fish swim.

Some people swim.

Some people are fish.

f. *Conclusion:* It's false that all paper is white.

Valid. This is an example of using deductive reasoning to refute a generalization.

g. *Conclusion:* The telephone book advertising pages are not white.

Invalid

Refuting analogy:

If the telephone book advertising pages are not yellow, then it's false that all paper is yellow; and it is false that all paper is yellow. So the telephone book advertising pages are not yellow.

6. a. Unsound, because invalid

b. Unsound, because invalid. It's also possible that some dogs do not bark and that some cats do not meow.

c. Unsound, because invalid. It's also possible that not all dogs bark.

d. Unsound, because it has at least one unacceptable support. President Clinton is not the chair of the philosophy department at. . . .

e. Unsound, because invalid. It's also possible that some beagles do not bark.

f. Sound. The argument is valid and has acceptable supports.

g. Unsound, because invalid

CHAPTER 8
THINKING THROUGH ANALOGIES

This chapter teaches students how to evaluate analogies used in explanations and how to identify and evaluate analogies used to support predictions, evaluations, and legal decisions.

SUMMARY

Analogies are comparisons and can serve a variety of purposes, such as helping us generate, organize, and explain ideas; label and categorize things; arouse indignation; and create laughter. This chapter focuses on the role of analogies to explain complex, abstract, or unfamiliar things and to support predictions, evaluations, and legal decisions. When you are using analogies to explain, take the audience into consideration by choosing analogies they can understand and by informing them of important similarities and differences between the things being compared.

Analogies used to support predictions link something we have experience about (the taste of last year's apples) to something we have not yet experienced (the taste of this year's apples). By finding comparisons between last year's apples and this year's apples, the reasoner concludes that the taste of this year's apples will be like the taste of last year's apples.

Analogies are frequently not explicitly stated, and it's useful to make them explicit so we can check their strength. To check the strength of an analogy, we look for relevant similarities and differences. We're not looking for just any similarities and differences, but similarities (the apples come from the same tree) that support the argument's conclusion and differences (picked from the tree versus picked from the ground) that would undermine the argument's conclusion. Background knowledge plays an important role in determining which similarities and differences are relevant.

The acceptability of a conclusion about the future depends on the acceptability of the statement about the past. If last year's apples weren't sweet or crisp, then a strong analogy won't make the prediction acceptable. We show our uncertainty about the future by adding words like "probably," "very likely, " or "might." We cannot make predictions from disanalogies between the past and future without assuming that other things will remain the same.

The analogies we use when supporting evaluations take us from one evaluation to another. Refuting analogies—which draw comparisons between arguments to show invalidity—are analogies that support evaluative conclusions. We also draw comparisons between situations, things, and people to make aesthetic and moral evaluations.

Once again, in a strong argument from analogy there are no relevant differences between the things being compared, and the starting point of the analogy is acceptable. We need to beware of adopting false models (confusing media-generated celebrity for heroism). But we may begin with a fanciful example (a science fiction story).

We make an invidious contrast when we find a *difference* between ourselves and a model and conclude that because we are not like the model, there's something wrong with us. This type of reasoning is fallacious. It assumes the model we've compared ourselves with is the *only possible* model, and there are typically several or many possible models of artistic or moral merit. Advertisements encourage us to draw invidious contrasts with the models in their ads so we will buy their products.

Legal reasoners make repeated use of the argument from analogy to support legal decisions. Like everyday analogical reasoning, strong legal analogical reasoning requires that the things compared must be relevantly similar and have no relevant differences. Unlike everyday analogical reasoning, legal analogical reasoning begins with a previously decided case, called a "precedent."

According to the doctrine of *stare decisis*, which means "let the decision stand," lawyers and judges are expected to use precedents even if they personally disagree with them. However, precedents are sometimes overturned when they're found to be inconsistent with other values implicit in the law.

Sometimes legal reasoners arrive at different decisions because they start with different precedents. The task is to determine which precedent is more relevant to the case in question.

COMMON PROBLEMS FOR STUDENTS

Students have considerable difficulty making implicit analogies explicit. Some have trouble seeing that a comparison is being made. Others state the comparison in very general terms.

When critiquing analogies, some students point to any difference at all between two things and think they've done the job of undermining the analogy. Often they don't have enough background knowledge about the subject of the argument to evaluate the analogy successfully. They need to become sensitive to the possibility that they lack sufficient background knowledge of the subject of the analogy to make a final evaluation of it. When writing papers, they need to be willing to do sufficient research on their topics to write strong arguments from analogy.

SAMPLE ANSWERS TO EXERCISES

1. Identifying comparisons:

    a. A comparison is made between a Tibetan hunter valuing a deer only for its (profitable) musk and a student valuing a teacher only for what the teacher can give the student.

    b. This excerpt from *Islands in the Street: Gangs and American Urban Society* compares the recruitment process of gangs to that of a college fraternity, equating the "trial period" of gangs to the "pledge period" of fraternities.

    c. The analogies in this piece compare an American family to a hard-boiled egg, Filipino families to scrambled eggs, and healthy families to fried eggs.

    d. Chief Tecumseh compares selling his country to selling air, clouds, and the sea.

    e. Charles Baron assumes that American treatment of African Americans is analogous to American treatment of Japanese Americans and German treatment of the Jews in the 1940s.

    f. Hawthorne uses a number of metaphors in his article. In the title he uses "train" metaphorically, implicitly comparing the civil rights movement to a train. In the first paragraph, Hawthorne refers to the fight for black rights as the "second civil war." In the third paragraph he compares affirmative action to a "Civil Rights Train out of control," ". . . madness in the form of social policies." He continues the analogy of the train in the concluding paragraph by saying, "stop this train we must." He also assumes that "preferences for whites" (1960s segregation laws) are analogous to "favoring blacks" (today's affirmative action policies).

    g. Chancellor Tien assumes a comparison between "elite private institutions giving special preferences to the children of alumni and of major donors" and "UC not using grade point averages and SAT scores as the sole determinant for admission." He also compares a future, divided, "two-tiered society" (the potential social effect of destroying University of California admissions requirements) with "those old buses" divided "along racial and ethnic lines" in the days of segregated buses.

    h. Richard Wasserstrom compares admitting only academically qualified students to universities with allowing only the best two players to use a community tennis court. In other words, he compares assuming a necessary connection between academic qualifications and deserving entry to college with assuming a necessary connection between tennis ability and deserving to use a community tennis court. Wasserstrom also assumes an analogy between "many jobs of substantial power and authority" and college.

  i. Justice Stewart compares the death sentence to being struck by lightning.

  j. Patricia J. Williams compares Mumia Abu-Jamal's book with Stacey Koon's book and G. Gordon Liddy's speech. She claims that if the First Amendment protected the latter two, it should also protect the former. Abu-Jamal compares life on death row to a "stressful psychic stew."

2. a. To explain and persuade. The writer expects the reader to find the student behavior as inappropriate as the hunter's behavior.

  b. To explain

  c. To explain

  d. To support the conclusion that a country cannot be sold

  e. To support the conclusion that African Americans are owed reparation

  f. The "train" and "second civil war" metaphors explain. The comparison of 1960s segregation laws with today's affirmation policies is used to support the conclusion that today's affirmative action policies are wrong.

  g. To support the conclusion that admission requirements in the California University system should not be revised.

  h. To support the conclusion that there's no necessary connection between academic qualifications and deserving to be admitted to college.

  i. To explain

  j. Williams's analogy is offered to support the conclusion that Abu-Jamal's book should be published. Abu-Jamal's metaphor is offered to explain.

3. Although the question didn't explicitly ask, students should begin by describing the starting points. Their answers evaluating these starting points will vary.

  a. The starting point is that Tibetan hunters value deer only for their musk. As Tulku is Tibetan, I assume he knows something of Tibetan hunters. However, whether Tibetan hunters actually see deer this way doesn't matter. The story is clear enough to serve as a starting point for an explanation.

  b. The description of fraternities is clear enough to serve as a useful starting point in an explanation.

c. The description of types of eggs is clear enough to serve as a useful starting point in an explanation.

d. The (implied) starting point here is that it's not possible to own or sell the air, clouds, and great sea or that we should not treat the air, clouds, and great sea as the property of individuals or groups. To the extent that countries set limits on who can and cannot own adjacent waters, countries are now "owning" seas. Perhaps we should not. Perhaps we should be sharing the sea with everyone. Tecumseh's starting point is controversial.

e. Baron's (implied) starting point is that Japanese Americans and Jews deserve reparations. I agree with Baron, the United States, and Germany in recognizing that reparations are deserved.

f. The image of the train is a clear one. Also, I accept the starting point of his argument: the 1960s segregation laws that favored whites were wrong.

g. Tien starts with the claim that people don't object that the admissions policies of elite private institutions that use criteria other than academic qualifications will cause a decline in academic quality. I don't know from my personal experience whether this claim is true. However, I consider Chancellor Tien an authority on this topic. I expect him to be in contact with people who would have access to this information, and I don't think he would lie about it, though he may be overstating it a bit. I'd be surprised if no one objected to the Ivy League policies, but perhaps there are not as many or they are not as vocal as those who object to UC policies.

h. The (implied) starting point is that there is no necessary connection between playing excellent tennis and deserving to play tennis at a community court.

i. The starting point is clear enough to serve in an explanation.

j. The starting point of Williams's argument is acceptable. Koon was permitted to publish and Liddy was permitted to speak. Answers will vary regarding the clarity of Abu-Jamal's metaphor.

4. Answers to this question will vary. Here are some possible responses.

a. I got the general idea of this comparison—that students, like Tibetan deer hunters, reduce the value of something to its worth for them. But potential differences tripped me up. The hunters kill the deer to get what they want. Do students in some way kill or harm the teacher when getting what they want? Also, the hunter can get what he wants (the musk) even if he doesn't value the deer as a whole, but the student presumably cannot. Genuine education requires that the student respect the teacher. Also, was the reference to buying the head of the teacher an implicit comparison with trophy hunting? I think Tulku's point is that focusing on what a teacher can give you leaves out an important part of education—namely, the student's active role in learning.

b. I don't find any sticking points here.

c. I don't find any sticking points here.

d. Land is easier to control than the air, clouds, and the sea; thus, it's possible to treat it as belonging to a group more easily than to treat air, clouds, and the sea as belonging to a group. I don't, however, find any differences that would rule out sharing them. However, Tucumseh's claim that they were all given to humans to share is controversial.

e. I'd need more background knowledge of the conditions under which reparations were given to Jews and Japanese Americans. Were the Jews and Japanese Americans receiving reparation for property that was taken away from them in Germany and in America? If so, can African Americans make similar claims to loss of property? Were they receiving reparations for the limits to their freedom imposed by being forced to enter "camps"? Slavery certainly imposed unfair limits to freedom for African American slaves.

f. Comparing affirmative action policies to a train out of control implies that no one is thinking through the policies, that they will damage those who use them and bystanders, and that there's nothing good about them. I'd need more evidence before accepting this controversial claim.

   I see some important differences between comparing the 1960s segregation laws with today's affirmative action policies. The main one is that the segregation laws reinforced the view that African Americans were in some way dirty or unworthy of equal treatment. Affirmative action policies do not have the same implications. Another difference is that affirmative action policies do not exclude all white males from admittance to education and jobs; segregation laws did exclude all African Americans from certain rights and privileges.

g. Tien makes his first comparison to lead his readers to the conclusion that they shouldn't be complaining that UC 's academic quality will decline because of its admissions practice. Whether his comparison of UC and Ivy League admissions policies works depends on whether the students let into UC are more likely to lower the academic standards than those allowed into the Ivy League. He needs to supply additional information for that claim. If he wants to use the comparison to make a moral point that UC policies are no more unfair than Ivy League policies, then the analogy works better.

h. Wasserstrom is making a very narrow point—that there's no necessary connection between academic qualifications and deserving to enter college. His analogy serves to make that point. But you'll have a hard time convincing students of it! Some discussion of the meaning of necessary connection would be useful.

i. This analogy implies that death sentences, like lightning strikes, are a random act of nature. If anything, the capriciousness of the death penalty is more related to systematic discrimination on the basis of race and class.

j. From the information that Williams gives about Koon, Liddy, and Abu-Jamal, I don't see a significant difference between the cases. But I do know that prisoners don't have the same rights to the freedom of expression as free citizens, so I'd like to know whether Koon published his book while he was still in prison.

5. Answers to this question will vary. Here are some possible responses.

a. An example of counterproductive behavior would better illustrate Tulku's point, I think. Killing the goose that lays the golden egg comes to mind. By respecting the goose, tending it, and caring for it, one has a better chance of getting the golden eggs. Another example of counterproductivity is trying to get nourishment by watching someone else eat and refusing to take up a spoon and fork oneself.

b. No need to answer if you didn't find a problem with the analogy.

c. It would be fun to extend this analogy and discuss different types of eggs. Poached eggs are a little less individualistic than hard boiled ones. And what about soft-boiled eggs? What happens to their centers when they're tapped into? There's plenty of room to play here. What types of families would be represented by coddled eggs, deviled eggs, or Eggs Benedict?

d. People who disagree with Tecumseh might say that land is more like moccasins than like the air; it is in a sense "man-made." Men can "mix their labor" with it, producing gardens that weren't there before.

e. No suggested answer

f. I recognize that affirmative action policies have some drawbacks, but I see merit in them. How about comparing affirmative action with taking a medicine that tastes bad? It leaves a temporary unpleasant taste in one's mouth, but it's useful for creating health in the long run. Affirmative action laws are more like preferences given to veterans in hiring.

g. No suggested answer

h. Wasserstrom might make his point more effectively by adding an example of things that are necessarily connected. There is a necessary connection between being a male and unmarried and qualifying for admission to a club for bachelors only. If having academic qualifications and being deserving were linked conceptually the way being male and unmarried are linked to being a bachelor, then there would be a necessary connection between academic qualifications and being deserving.

i. No suggested answer

j. No suggested answer

SAMPLE ANSWERS TO READINGS FOR ANALYSIS

Justices Fortas and Black, "Free Political Speech in Schools"

1. Mr. Justice Fortas notes that the school authorities did not attempt to "prohibit the wearing of all symbols of political or controversial significance." The school restricted wearing black armbands and did not restrict wearing political buttons and the "Iron Cross" symbol of Nazism. Fortas implies that wearing black armbands is analogous to wearing political buttons and the Iron Cross (an implicit comparison), so that if the school is consistent, it should restrict all or not restrict any. When criticizing the school officials' restriction of student speech, Fortas uses a metaphor, "closed-circuit recipients," that implicitly compares the students' situation in the school with electrical wiring.

   Mr. Justice Black uses the metaphor "wrecked" to implicitly compare the effects of wearing the armbands in the mathematics class to the destruction caused by an automobile collision or when a ship is dashed against a rocky shoreline. When he says "the next logical step . . . would be to hold unconstitutional laws that bar pupils under 21 or 18 from voting, or from being elected members of the boards of education . . ." he implies that permitting students under 18 to express their opinions by wearing black armbands is analogous to permitting them to vote or to being elected members of boards of education. By outlining the court case of *Waugh v. Mississippi University*, Mr. Justice Black uses the court case as a situation analogous to that of the situation in Iowa. He explicitly compares the purpose of education in Iowa and Mississippi: "Iowa's public schools, like Mississippi's university, are operated to give students an opportunity to learn, not to talk politics by actual speech, or by 'symbolic' speech. He assumes that armband speech in the Iowa school is analogous to fraternity membership in Mississippi.

2. Fortas's "closed-circuit" metaphor highlights the restrictive nature of the speech restriction. Fortas compares wearing black armbands with wearing political buttons and the Iron Cross to support the conclusion that the school policy singled out "one particular opinion." He couples this subconclusion with the lack of evidence that the armbands were substantially disruptive to support his conclusion that the prohibition is unconstitutional. (Another way of understanding Fortas here would be to take the lack of evidence that the armbands were substantially disruptive as support for the implicit analogy that wearing the black armbands is like wearing political buttons.)

   Black's "wrecked" metaphor highlights disruption caused by armband speech. Black compares permitting students under eighteen to express their opinions by wearing black armbands with permitting them to vote or to being elected members of the boards of education to support the implied conclusion that permitting the armband expression is inappropriate. He compares the purpose of education in Iowa and Mississippi and compares armband speech with fraternity membership to support his conclusion that Iowa's restriction is not unconstitutional.

3. More background information is needed to answer this question fully. We need to know whether any disruptions were caused at the school by the students' wearing the political buttons and Iron Cross. We also need to know what kinds of disruptions were caused by fraternity membership in Mississippi. And finally we need to know the seriousness of the disruptions. From my experience as a teacher, I know that students are constantly making faces at each other, cracking jokes, whispering, and in other ways using speech that in some way or another "disrupts" the class. Yet these disruptions usually don't warrant sending students home. I'd like to have more details about the armband disruption. Did it "wreck" the class or not? And I'd like to know the teacher's role. How teachers respond to student speech makes a big difference in whether these rocky places wreck a class or not. Maybe the teacher just wasn't a very good captain. As for the "closed-circuit" analogy, I'd call it an overstatement. Some teachers might wish they could control what students say and hear as effectively as they can control electrical wiring, but that's an impossible dream. Sparks are bound to fly when students—or any other awake and alert people—come together.

4. Provide more information in support of the comparisons drawn.

5. Student answers will vary. From living through the Vietnam era, I suspect that Fortas downplayed the extent to which the armband speech was disruptive. Nonetheless, I agree with the majority opinion that the armband speech should be permitted. I think teachers have responsibility in minimizing disruption, and I believe that schools should not only permit but encourage student discussion of

such issues. Students right out of high school were being drafted to risk their lives and kill others in that war. It seems crucial, therefore, that they have the opportunity to think through their attitudes toward it.

6. Student answers will vary. Some schools prohibit wearing gang-related clothing. Some schools have instituted uniforms. Prohibiting the wearing of gang-related clothing protects the lives of students who otherwise are mistaken for gang members. Wearing uniforms protects from insults and humiliation students who cannot afford designer labels. In neither case is the restriction designed to prohibit significant political speech.

7. Student answers will vary.

Justices Kennedy and Scalia, "The Constitutionality of Drug Testing"

1. Justice Kennedy implicitly compares urine tests of drug-interdicting or firearm-carrying Customs employees with routine searches of U.S. Mint employees and the seemingly "extraordinary assurances of trustworthiness and probity" and "intrusive inquiries into physical fitness" of applicants for military or intelligence services. He also compares the small incidence of discovered wrongdoing among drug-tested Customs employees with the incidence of discovered wrongdoing among homeowners subject to housing code inspections (permitted by *Camera v. Municipal Court*) and motorists stopped at approved checkpoints (permitted by *United States v. Martinez-Fuerte*).

   Justice Antonin Scalia notes a disanalogy between testing Customs Service employees and searching prisoners (permitted by *Bell v. Wolfish*) and searching railroad employees involved in train accidents (*Skinner*). He compares drug-using Customs Service employees with those wearing diamonds and with speeding police officers. He also compares drug testing of Customs Service employees with random stops to check drivers' licenses and motor vehicle registration (prohibited by *Delaware v. Prouse*).

2. Kennedy uses the Customs/U.S. Mint/military analogy to support the implied conclusion that U.S. Customs employees should expect to be subject to drug testing. He uses the Customs employees/homeowners/motorists analogy to support the conclusion that the infrequency of discovered wrongdoing should not stand in the way of drug testing.

   Scalia uses a disanalogy between testing Customs officials and prisoners or railroad employees involved in train accidents to support the conclusion that drug testing of Customs officials should not be permitted. He compares drug-using Customs employees with diamond-wearing Customs employees and speeding police officers to support the conclusion that Customs officials won't fail to be "sympathetic" to their drug-interdiction mission. He uses the Customs employee/drivers' license analogy to support the conclusion that drug testing should be prohibited.

3. I'd like to see more information provided about why invasions of privacy are allowed in the case of the U.S. Mint and the military before I would agree that similar reasons exist for Customs employees. One possible difference between the homeowner and Customs employees' cases is that employees typically have supervisors who judge their performance. The employer can discipline on the basis of the behavior without doing a drug test. However, in the case of the homeowner, there's no government official around on a consistent basis to note and penalize persons who do dangerously poor construction nor will such construction be evident when the building is complete until the building fails in some way.

A potential relevant difference occurs in Scalia's analogy of the drug-using Customs employee and the diamond-wearing one. One might expect law-breaking officials to be more sympathetic to smugglers than non-law-breaking officials would be. As if anticipating this objection, Scalia adds another analogy, the speeding cop, and so ends up comparing two lawbreakers.

Kennedy and Scalia both use motorists' cases as starting points for analogies to justify their positions regarding drug testing of Customs employees. As you try to decide which of the cases is more analogous, it would be useful to have more information about the cases. But in any case, permitting a car search doesn't strike me as sufficiently similar to testing a person's urine to allow for the latter when the former is permitted. As Scalia points out, the search of a person is far more intrusive than the search of a car. You'd have to have a much stronger reason for searching a person than for searching a car.

4. I need more background knowledge about the cases cited and the situation of Customs officials to make a final decision about the analogies offered.

5. No right answer. I tend to support Justice Scalia. It's not clear to me why some of the illegal drugs are illegal in the first place. I don't see some of them as any more dangerous than alcohol, and so I don't know why a person's privacy should be violated to check for drug use (unless it were also going to be violated to check for alcohol use). Furthermore, if supervisors can't tell from the behavior of the employee that the employee is on drugs, then testing doesn't provide any useful information about employee performance. It only tells the supervisor that the employee has done something illegal (assuming that the test was not a false positive).

6. There is no right answer to this question.

COMMENTS ON WRITING IDEAS

The first writing assignment gives students the opportunity to practice producing analogies in explanations. You could ask students to do some research, looking through texts for their other classes or paying close attention to lectures to find analogies to write about.

The next two writing assignments ask students to write arguments from analogy. The fourth writing idea gives students the opportunity to critique analogies in the Supreme Court cases.

The last writing assignment would be a good one for a short in-class freewrite and class discussion. Here I give students a chance to add their own ideas about analogical thinking.

CLASSROOM ACTIVITIES

Creating Analogies

Description: Students pick abstract concepts that they want to explain to each other, then do some looping freewrites that begin ". . . is like . . ." to see what they come up with. Students read their freewrites to the class, and the class selects several analogies as ones they find most useful in explaining the concepts.

Purpose: To develop the ability to think creatively

To learn to critique analogies used to explain abstract concepts

To develop the ability to work constructively with others

Debating with Arguments from Analogy

Description: Students form teams and present arguments in favor of and opposed to a position taken in one of the above readings for analysis (or Frederick Turner's "Speech to a Woman Seeking an Abortion," a reading for analysis in Chapter 2). They present their arguments to the class. The students in the audience point out potential relevant differences between the things being compared and take a vote on which side presented the strongest analogy. A student moderator facilitates the presentation and following discussion, making sure the presenters do not go over their time limit and that all who want to speak in the audience have a chance to do so.

Purpose: To develop analytic skills

To improve speaking skills

To learn to apply concepts for critiquing arguments from analogy

Students exchange papers they have written using analogies and critique each other's analogies.

Comparing Exercise Answers

Description: Select several examples from the exercises for students to work on in groups. Then ask the students to report their answers back to the class.

Purpose: To develop the ability to recognize and critique analogies

To develop the ability to think for oneself

To develop the ability to work productively with others

QUIZ ITEMS AND ANSWERS

1. True/False

   a. Because there are always some differences between two things being compared you have to find relevant differences between the things being compared to establish that the analogy isn't successful in achieving its purpose.

   b. When using an analogy to explain something, it's a good idea to start with something your audience is familiar with.

   c. When you're using an analogy to explain something and you find some difference between the things being compared, you should just throw out the analogy and find another one.

   d. When critiquing arguments, don't worry too much about implicit analogies. They tend to be strong ones.

   e. For an argument from a claim about a past event to work to establish a claim about a future one, the past event must be appropriately similar to the future one.

f. In analogies used to support predictions, whether a difference is relevant or not is pretty obvious on the face of it.

g. You can never improve an argument from analogy by adding "probably" to the conclusion.

h. Though you can make predictions from analogies, you can never make them from disanalogies.

i. According to the text, you should never use fanciful models as starting points of evaluative arguments.

j. According to David Shaw, celebrity and heroism are not the same thing.

k. According to the text, advertisers discourage invidious contrasts.

l. Analogical reasoning in the law is exactly the same as analogical reasoning in everyday life.

2. Short answer

a. Define "relevant difference."

b. Define "precedent."

c. What is the doctrine of *stare decisis*?

d. What are two questions to ask yourself when critiquing an analogy used in an explanation?

3. Read this passage and answer the questions following.

Mary: Women shouldn't try to save money by washing their hair before going to get a haircut. They don't take salads to restaurants to save money. (Paraphrase of an example in Howard Kahane, *Logic and Contemporary Rhetoric*, 3rd ed. [Belmont, CA: Wadsworth, 1980] 65.)

a. Does this passage contain an explanation of a concept or an argument? Explain, stating the concept being explained or the conclusion of the argument.

b. What two things are being implicitly or explicitly compared?

c. Describe any relevant similarities and differences you find.

d. Describe a closer analogy than the one offered.

4. Read this passage and answer the questions following.

> Many parents worry about any mistake they make, but they shouldn't be so hard on themselves. In baseball, batting 300 is considered excellent. And yet when batting 300, one misses twice as many times as one hits. With parenting, we tend to miss a lot too. But if we score ourselves the way ball players do, we will recognize we are good parents as long as we do something right at least one out of three times.

    a. What implicit or explicit analogy is made in this passage?

    b. What is the purpose of this analogy?

    c. Does the analogy succeed in achieving its purpose?

5. In commenting on a decision made by a 10-month-old boy's parents not to allow treatment for his leukemia but instead to place their faith in God for a cure, Baruch Brody begins his comment with the following paragraph.

> I must confess that I have little sympathy for the parents' decision. Coming from a Jewish theological background, I find their position objectionable on theological grounds. The objection was best put by Rabbis Akiva and Ishmael when they said: "Just as if one does not weed, fertilize, and plow, the trees will not produce, and if fruit is produced but is not watered or fertilized it will not live but die, so with regard to the body. Drugs and medicines are the fertilizer and the physician is the tiller of the soil." It is strange to find people actively intervening throughnatural means to produce desired results in all areas but matters of life and death, and insisting that in those areas alone man should merely pray and leave himself in the hands of God.[1]

    a. What implicit or explicit analogy is contained in this passage?

    b. What is the purpose of the analogy?

    c. Are there any differences relevant to undermining the analogy? What additional background would be useful to you in answering this question?

---

[1] Baruch Brody, "Commentary," in *Cases in Bioethics: Selections from the Hastings Center Report*, 2nd ed., Bette-Jane Crigger, ed., St. Martin's Press, 1993, p. 34. Copyright © 1993 St. Martin's Press. Reprinted by permission.

6. In *Schenck v. United States* in 1919, Justice Holmes wrote, "The most stringent protection of free speech would not protect a man in falsely shouting fire in a theater and causing a panic." Suppose you agree with Justice Holmes. Is the following speech analogous enough to conclude that it is also not protected speech? Explain.

> During World War I, Charles Schenck, general secretary of the Socialist party, printed and distributed 15,000 leaflets urging resistance to the draft.

Answers

1. True/False

   a. True
   b. True
   c. False
   d. False
   e. True
   f. False. You often need background information to determine relevancy.
   g. False
   h. False
   i. False
   j. True
   k. False
   l. False

2. Short Answer

   a. In an explanation using an analogy, a difference between the things being compared that distracts an audience from understanding the subject being explained. In an argument from analogy, a difference between the things being compared that undermines the claim that if something's true of the first thing it is also true of the second.

   b. In law, a previously decided case used to guide decisions about future similar cases.

   c. In law, the doctrine that decisions about past cases stand firm and guide future similar cases unless the past decisions are found to conflict with basic principles of justice.

    d. Is the starting point of the analogy familiar to the audience? Are any of the differences between the things being compared likely to distract the audience (or are there any relevant differences between the things being compared)?

3. a. This passage is an argument. The conclusion is "Women shouldn't try to save money by washing their own hair before going to get a haircut."

    b. Saving money by washing hair before getting a haircut is being compared with taking a salad to a restaurant.

    c. There is a one similarity between washing hair before going to get a haircut and taking a salad to a restaurant. Both are attempts by a customer to save money at the expense of a business.

       The author compares eating a salad *at a restaurant* with washing one's hair *before* going to get a haircut. This difference is relevant to undermining the analogy's strength because someone could well object to a person's bringing salad to a restaurant and *not* object to a person's washing her hair before having it cut. (There is another difference between the things being compared. One business provides food services; the other provides hair services. This difference is not relevant to undermining the analogy's purpose.)

    d. A closer analogy to eating one's homemade salad at a restaurant to save money would be shampooing one's hair or snipping off pieces of one's own hair *at the beauty shop* and expecting to be charged less as a result. A closer analogy to shampooing one's hair *before* having it cut would be eating a salad *before* going to a restaurant.

4. a. That parenting is like baseball batting

    b. This analogy is offered to support the conclusion that a person can make a mistake two out of three times and still be a good parent. Offered to relieve a parent's anxiety about making mistakes. (Another interpretation of this analogy is that it's explaining the concept of "good" in "good parent.")

    c. I find this comparison useful for reminding myself that figuring out what a growing and changing child needs, like hitting a ball moving 90 miles an hour, is very hard to do. This analogy helps me avoid using an unreasonably high standard of success. However, I also realize there is a big difference between playing ball and parenting. If you have a bad batting day, all you risk losing is a ball game; but if you have a bad parenting day, you risk losing your child.

5. a. That medicines are like fertilizers and physicians are like farmers

   b. To support the conclusion that it's OK to treat leukemia medically (there's something odd about or wrong with the parents' refusal to allow medical treatment for their child).

   c. As the parents are refusing treatment for spiritual reasons, they might believe there is a spiritual difference between plants and humans. The meaning of death and how one dies is different for plants than for humans. Also, fertilizer is more like vitamins than like leukemia treatment. If a plant had a life-threatening illness, fertilizer would not be a recommended treatment. Additional background about the side effects of leukemia treatment could present other relevant differences between it and fertilizing plants. Finally, additional background about the meaning of "place their faith in God for a cure" would be useful. Are the parents praying for a cure? Are they or religious healers doing anything else? Is there any evidence about the effectiveness of prayer and religious healings?

6. That would depend on whether printing and distributing leaflets would be likely to cause the kind of panic, immediate action, and injuries that shouting "fire" in a crowded theater would cause. I suspect that it would not. People could look at the leaflets and think about their content. They wouldn't be so likely to automatically and immediately react, the way people do when they fear they will be burned to death. It also depends on whether the claims made are equally unacceptable. A person who falsely cries "fire" in a crowded theater subjects others to injury for no good reason. Persons who argue for draft resistance could be basing their conclusions on acceptable support. People who act on their speech may be avoiding unnecessary harm to themselves and others.

CHAPTER 9
GENERATING GENERALIZATIONS

This chapter teaches students how to distinguish between precisely and imprecisely stated generalizations and how to evaluate generalizations derived from samples or based on claims of common knowledge or expertise.

SUMMARY

A generalization is a claim about individuals in a group or class. Understanding how to generate generalizations is important for making decisions, because generalizations help us make predictions about the world. And we use predictions when we make decisions.

To reason effectively from generalizations, we need to note the scope of the generalization, qualify the conclusion we make from our generalization (adding probably or possibly, if appropriate), and make sure the generalization we began with is acceptable.

Some generalizations are broad, such as "All feral cats eat birds." Others are more narrow: "Some feral cats eat birds." Generalizations with numbers, such as "75% of feral cats eat birds," are called *statistical generalizations*. Some generalizations contain weasel words ("up to" or "at least some"). Broad generalizations that are overstated are called *glittering generalizations*, *sweeping generalizations*, or *blanket generalizations*. Stereotypes are false or misleading generalizations that state or imply negative or positive judgments.

You can arrive at acceptable generalizations in a number of ways: observing the entire group, relying on the word of a candid and knowledgeable authority, and using common knowledge. We can also observe or interview a small part (sample) and make inferences about the whole (population) from what we learn about the small part. When we want to know if the soup has enough pepper, for example, we taste a spoonful and generalize to the whole pot.

If we are to make accurate generalizations about a population from studying a sample, the sample must be representative of (analogous to) the population. Some sample designs that result in representative samples include the simple random sample, the multistage sampling design, and the stratified random sample.

Biased (unrepresentative) samples occur when you sample "birds of a feather"—for example, man-in-the-street interviews. Salespeople sometimes create biased samples to mislead customers. And people tend to overgeneralize from vivid but biased personal experience.

Once a sample is large enough to contain the possible variables in the population, increasing sample size does not significantly increase sample representativeness. When the population is relatively uniform, a very small sample can be representative of it. However, people should watch out for assuming that a group is uniform merely because the group is called by one name.

When trying to decide whether a sample is likely to be representative of its population, ask yourself the following questions:

1. Was the pot stirred before you tasted it? (Is the sample random?)

2. Are there any signs of sample bias?

   a. Is the sample filled with floating vegetables? (Are the individuals in the sample "birds of a feather flocking together"?)

   b. Did a soup salesman create the sample? (Is the sample likely to result from crafty sample selection?)

   c. Was the sample a vivid but potentially unrepresentative, personal experience?

3. Is the tasting spoon large enough to contain all the vegetables in the soup? (Is the sample large enough to contain the full range of variables in the population in the correct proportions?)

4. Were all the cookies cut from the same mold? (Are the individuals in the population enough alike that one of them can represent the rest? Does the group's common name blanket individual differences?)

There is one more thing to take into account when making generalizations, whether you are observing the entire group or only a part of it. You must obtain accurate information about the individuals you observed or interviewed.

Researchers frequently use polls or surveys or interviews to obtain information about humans, but questioning does not always yield the knowledge the researcher seeks. Many factors influence the completeness and accuracy of information obtained from questioning, including the subject's self-knowledge, the subject's candor, neutral or loaded questions, the questioner, the breadth of questions, and precise or vague questions.

Statisticians typically qualify the conclusions of their research by stating the margin of error and the confidence level for the study. The margin of error states how far off the figures in the population are likely to be from the figures in the sample. The confidence level states the statisticians' degree of confidence that the percentages sought for the population will fall within the reported margin of error. In order to draw a conclusion about a population from the sample, you must know the margin of error for the study.

COMMON PROBLEMS FOR STUDENTS

Background knowledge plays a role in student ability to recognize potential sample bias. If students are aware of variables not contained in the sample, they recognize bias. If not, they do not. They tend to find counterintuitive the notion that sampling at random increases representativeness, but they learn it nonetheless. They tend not to recognize that they themselves frequently make generalizations from vivid and biased personal experience, so it's important to discuss examples of generalizations we make from our personal contacts. The mathematics involved in using a margin of error to compute percentages for a population are easy, and students enjoy learning to make these simple and important calculations.

SAMPLE ANSWERS TO EXERCISES

1. a. Generalization
   b. Statistical generalization
   c. Generalization
   d. Generalization
   e. Statistical generalization
   f. Not a generalization
   g. Not a generalization
   h. Generalization
   i. Generalization
   j. Not a generalization
   k. Generalization
   l. Generalization
   m. Statistical generalization
   n. Generalization

2. Examples of blanket generalizations are c, h, i, k, l, and n. Examples of stereotypes (exaggerated and potentially damaging generalizations) are found in c, i, and n. Examples of weaselers are found in b ("at least"), e ("up to"), m ("as few as").

3. a. *Sample:* The restaurants Lee Ross took Richard Nisbett to in Palo Alto.

   Population: All the restaurants in Palo Alto.

   Nisbett is also making a generalization about Ann Arbor restaurants, perhaps on the basis of his experience there and on the basis of other witness reports.

   b. *Sample:* The single prison tour is a sample.

   Population: The conditions at the prison 24 hours a day, seven days a week

   c. *Sample:* The attitudes of the incoming class at Harvard

   Population: The attitudes of all college students

   d. *Sample:* The individuals chosen at random from the male and female students

   Population: All the students on the list are the population.

   e. *Sample:* The white sorority women selected at random

   Population: All college-aged women

   f. *Sample:* The students who answered the questions on the way into the game

   Population: All students on campus

4. *Stratified random sample:* Example d. is an example of this strategy. The school population was broken into strata (the groups of men and women), then individuals were chosen at random from each stratum. None of the other examples used reliable sampling designs.

5. a. The sample is biased because Ross is likely to take Nisbett to Palo Alto restaurants that Ross thinks Nisbett will like, not to a random sample of them. The selection was probably not crafty. Ross wasn't trying to trick Nisbett—just trying to be a good host.

   b. The sample is biased. There's the possibility of crafty sample selection here. The prison officials could have arranged that the visitors saw no brutality on the day they came.

   c. The sample is biased. Students who attend Harvard can be expected to have more money than students in general. That variable difference could affect the outcome.

   e. The sample is biased. Only one race is included in the sample.

   f. The sample is biased. People who attend the game are birds of a feather flocking together. They're more likely to give a high priority to funding the athletic program than the population as a whole.

6. a. It encourages candid answers by implying that soap opera watching is common.

   b. It's vague. How many is frequently, rarely?

   c. Loaded, with a reason against international students watching soap operas

   d. Loaded, with a reason for international students watching soap operas

   e. Open ended; allows for individual answers.

   f. Open ended, allows for individual answers. It could also be vague, if students have no common agreement about what critical thinking is.

   g. It encourages a candid answer by implying that waiting until the last minute is a common phenomenon.

   h. Loaded with a reason for making critical thinking a requirement.

   i. Vague, as students probably have different understandings of critical thinking. It also may tend to get yes answers, assuming that people think using critical thinking is a good thing.

   j. Loaded; implies that all students think critical thinking is a waste of time.

7. All the questions are open to different interpretations by different students, making them ineffective as a tool for determining a teacher's value. There's no set right answer regarding how to get more information. But some ideas include asking open-ended questions; asking students to define what they mean by "fair," "intellectually stimulating," "creativity," or to give examples of teacher behavior to support their evaluations; ask more precise questions, like "How many times did the teacher not appear at class on time?" or "How many times did the teacher offer to meet with students who could not come to office hours?" or "What percentage of the time did the teacher return papers within a week?"

8. The following answers include some considerations. You may think of others.

   a. Potentially awkward. Many students may not feel comfortable being candid in a one-on-one confrontation.

   b. Potentially awkward. Many students may not feel comfortable being candid in front of the entire class.

   c. Biased. These students are doing well already and though they may have input, what they have to say may not benefit those students who are struggling with the material.

    d. Potentially useful, if the questions are not loaded or vague and include some that are open ended.

    e. Potentially useful, if the other person is an experienced interviewer and the students trust the person

    f. Biased for reasons similar to those in c

    g. Potentially biased

9. None of the surveys discuss sample size, margin of error, confidence level, or sponsorship, although a. and b. do cite Gallup (a well-known poll taker) as the source. Examples c. and d. do not cite the source of the information (who conducted the survey). Without knowing sample size or source, someone reading the survey results will have difficulty feeling confident in the numbers given.

10. a. The people are asked to report their own attitudes. They're witnesses. How reliable they are depends on how much self-knowledge they have. They may have some wishful thinking about their own values.

    b. The people polled are presumably not experts, just average folks. But it would take a reliable expert to provide any useful information about the questions asked. Otherwise, people are likely to make generalizations from their own biased samples. Also, the example doesn't tell the ages of the adults polled. If they were young people twenty years ago, they may be engaging in a bit of historical revisionism.

    c. It's hard to tell what is required to be an expert or witness on the subject of the American national character; the concept is so vague. Perhaps it could be defined in such a way that one needed no special training or education to determine whether it had changed. The persons polled presumably have no particular expertise about the American character, but I find their answers worthless not because they are not experts, but because the question asked is hopelessly vague.

    d. Once again, there's no information given that suggests the persons polled have knowledge or experience relevant to answering the question asked.

SAMPLE ANSWERS TO READINGS FOR ANALYSIS

"Majority Opposes Clinton's Smoking Crackdown"

1. a. is a conclusion; b. is not. Another conclusion is that there's relatively weak support for the premise behind Clinton's proposed regulations. The author's statements "Fifty-eight percent reject . . ." and "And 53 percent oppose . . ." are also conclusions. Following the introductory paragraph, which refers to the population (not the sample), these claims appear to be about the population. If so, the figures given are too precise (unless the margin of error is 0).

2. Presumably it's American adults; but this is not explicitly stated.

3. 1,007 adults

4. This article has a number of glitches. First, no margin of error or confidence level is reported. We are also not told who conducted the study. Presumably the Associated Press sponsored it. Assuming a margin of error of +/- 3%, the numbers given do not support the conclusion. The largest percentage in opposition to one of Clinton's proposals is 58%. It's already an exaggeration to label 58% "most," but using the margin of error, the percentage of the population could be as low as 55%. The author also bases the conclusion that there is relatively weak support for the premise behind the regulations on the claim that 40% agree unequivocally about tobacco company motivations. Did other people agree, but not *unequivocally*? If so, the support for the premise behind the regulations may be stronger than the article implies.

5. I'd like to know what the Associated Press's politics are and the degree to which they depend on advertising, including tobacco advertising, for their income. As written, the article is slanted against regulating tobacco advertising. I wonder if the Associated Press intentionally withheld information gained in the study that would have created the impression of stronger support for regulations. I also wonder whether any of the questions were loaded.

6. The people polled apparently have no expertise on the subject of tobacco advertising, but they need some expertise to give informed answers to the questions.

7. The headline says "majority opposes . . ." yet the first sentence says that most Americans oppose "some of . . ." I wonder if in fact a majority oppose all of or even most of the proposed regulations. The word "crackdown" is also worth noting. It sounds as if anyone violating the proposed regulations will meet with serious penalties.

"Poll—State Voters Back Execution 4–1"

1. a. Amnesty International and the American Civil Liberties Union (ACLU) are devoted to protecting Human Rights. I don't know the *Los Angeles Times* values.

    b. Amnesty International and the American Civil Liberties Union oppose the death penalty. I don't know whether the *Los Angeles Times* has a public stand on the death penalty.

2. The exact wording of all questions was not made available. Exact wording is important to know because how a question is asked can influence the answers given by respondents. The article does report that 67% favored life imprisonment when murderers were required to work in prison to pay their victims. This suggests that the Amnesty International/American Civil Liberties Union question about life imprisonment was loaded with a reason for this sentence. We aren't given enough information to know whether the *Los Angeles Times* poll contained loaded questions.

3. The sample for the *Times* survey was defined as "registered voters." The Amnesty/ACLU sample was not defined.

4. a. The population for the *Times* survey was labeled "California voters." We have no information regarding the labels placed on the Amnesty/ACLU survey sample and population. It's important to check the labels to see whether a conclusion drawn from a sample actually fits the information in the sample.

    b. The headline reads "State voters." Checking the label in the headline matters for the same reason it matters to compare the sample and population labels. You want to see whether the headline makes a broader claim than is justified by the sample.

5. Sample size is given for the *Times* survey only: 1,667. Considering the number of registered voters in the state of California, this would be considered adequate.

6. If you compare the numbers from the sample of those who support Harris's execution and those who oppose, you get about 4/1.

    a. If you include the margin of error and if you count those who are not sure as not backing Harris's execution, the difference is closer to 3/1. In any case, there are many more supporting the execution than not. There are also many more supporting execution in general, though at most 2/1, not 4/1.

    b. The Amnesty/ACLU survey directly contradicts the *Times* survey. Oddly, the newspaper article says the Amnesty/ACLU survey "contrasted somewhat" with the *Los Angeles Times* finding.

7. "Two-Thirds of Public Favor Life Imprisonment for Murder"

8. "Public Commitment to Death Penalty in Question"

9. No right answer

Jin K. Kim, "American Self-Advertising"

1. That a lack of self-assertion is interpreted as timidity and a lack of self-confidence. In America, self-promotion is encouraged to the point of pretentiousness.

2. Yes. He claims that the entire American culture fits his generalizations.

3. Kim's support is in the form of personal experience in witnessing the behaviors of others.

4. Although he has a Ph.D. and is a professor at a university, his area of expertise is not listed as American Cultural Studies.

5. No right answer

6. No right answer

7. No right answer

Catherine McHugh Engstrom and William E. Sedlacek, "A Study of Prejudice toward University Student-Athletes"

1. The authors are interested in learning about student attitudes toward student athletes.

2. Via random sample of freshmen

3. By failing to quantify the percentage of students who expressed feelings of resentment, the surveyors create an overly broad generalization. (The original article included more specific numerical data.) They also make the broad generalizations that freshmen "think in dualistic ways" and "the more information

we have about a particular group, the more comfortable and safe we are talking about the group . . ."

4. They use their survey results to support the first claim. They reference other experts for the second and third claims.

5. Yes. Their credentials imply that they have experience and expertise with this population.

6. Decisions about addressing prejudice on college campuses

7. There is no right answer to this question.

COMMENTS ON WRITING IDEAS

The first writing exercise gives students an opportunity to put their critical thinking into action. Ideally, they will select a poll or survey reported in their local newspaper and send their letter to the newspaper for publication. The second exercise gives students an opportunity to educate others about generalizations. Students have reported to me that they enjoy sharing their new awareness of stereotypes with family and friends.

The third writing idea gives students another opportunity to rethink and rework papers they have written, using the new information in this chapter. The fourth helps them learn to distinguish stronger from weaker survey questions. The fifth exercise gives them a chance, once again, to add their own ideas to the class. It would make a good freewrite for class discussion.

CLASSROOM ACTIVITIES

Evaluating Generalizations about Students and Professors

Description: Students list some commonly held generalizations about college students and college professors on the board. The class selects one or two for study and takes a few minutes to list personal experiences and other information that is relevant to confirming or disconfirming the generalizations. The class votes on whether they agree, disagree, or withhold judgment about the selected generalizations.

The class then divides into groups, each group taking one of the following tasks.

Identify any difficulties in getting to know the individual students and professors.

Determine how to produce a representative sample of students and faculty to study.

Identify any vivid (and unduly influential) data offered on the board to support or reject the generalizations.

Each group makes a report to the class. The class votes again on whether they agree, disagree, or withhold judgment about the selected generalizations.

Purpose: To develop the ability to question generalizations

To develop skills for generating accurate generalizations

To develop respect for others

To develop the ability to work productively with others

Questions and Answers about Exercises

Description: Students form three groups. Two of them take turns asking each other questions about selected exercises. The third group (with the help of the instructor) decides whether the answers are satisfactory.

Purpose: To develop the ability to ask relevant questions

To learn concepts used in evaluating generalizations

To develop listening and speaking skills

Developing Survey Questions

Description: The class selects a population for study and discusses what information they want from the population. The class then divides into groups and each group makes a quick list of stronger and weaker interview questions. Two members of each group are sent to the other group to critique the questions. The groups then evaluate their visitors' answers with the instructor standing by to help resolve disputes. Afterward, the class holds a general discussion on what they learned about generating and critiquing interview questions.

Purpose: To develop the ability to identify vague questions and write precise ones

To develop the ability to identify loaded questions and write unloaded ones

To develop the ability to identify and generate open-ended questions

To develop the ability to generate questions that elicit candid responses

To develop the ability to work constructively with others

To develop the capacity to think for oneself

Using Personal Experiences to Counteract Stereotypes

Description: Students write freewrites on their personal experiences of being stereotyped and how those stereotypes do not apply to them. They then read their freewrites to each other in small groups. Afterward, the class meets as a whole to discuss the stereotyping and how to compensate for its negative effects.

Purposes: To develop writing skills

To develop creative thinking

To develop emotional health

To develop respect for others

To improve self-esteem and self-confidence

QUIZ ITEMS AND ANSWERS

1. True/False

   a. _____ "Most dogs bark" is a narrower generalization than "All dogs bark."

   b. _____ As a rule, you won't find weasel words in generalizations.

   c. _____ Some generalizations are called "glittering" because they're as true as diamonds.

d. _____ When you make a prediction from a generalization, it helps to state the generalization precisely.

e. _____ Some generalizations are acceptable on the basis of common knowledge.

f. _____ When you are reading a report of a study, it's useful to know who conducted the study, but you don't need to know who sponsored it.

g. _____ People have a tendency to use their own vivid personal experiences as biased samples for generalizations.

h. _____ A small sample is always biased.

i. _____ Sometimes we overlook differences among individuals in a group, in part because we have labeled the group.

j. _____ Sometimes people being surveyed don't give accurate information about their personal experience because they don't know themselves very well or because they are embarrassed.

k. _____ When you are preparing interviews of subjects, it's important to figure out a list of good questions because then you don't have to worry about who asks the questions.

l. _____ The confidence level tells you how confident the interviewer is that the subjects questioned gave reliable answers to the questions asked.

2. Short Answer

   a. Give an example of a biased sample. Explain why you say it is biased.

   b. Give an example of a loaded question. Explain why you say it is loaded.

   c. What is a census?

3. Match the Following

   a. sample, b. simple random sample, c. census, d. multistage sampling design, e. stratified random sample, f. sponsor, g. representative, h. population, i. whole group, j. sampling birds of a feather, k. crafty sample selection, l. survey conductor, m. margin of error, n. probability.

   a. _____ The group or organization that paid to have a study done.

   b. _____ Tells you how far off the figures in the population are likely to be from the figures in the sample.

c. _____ The entire group a researcher seeks information about by studying a part of it.

d. _____ A sample design you will have if you put the names of all college students into a hat, toss the names around until they are completely mixed up, then select some one by one.

e. _____ A sample design you will have if you put the names of all male college students in one hat and the names of all female college students in another hat, mix up the names in the hats, then select individual names from the hats.

f. _____ What you would have if you interviewed a random sample of people standing in line to watch *Pulp Fiction* to find out about American attitudes toward violence in the media.

g. _____ A real-estate salesman who knows you love to surf and wants you to move to Northern California shows you coastal property only on days when the surf is high.

h. _____ A sample that is like its population.

4. Suppose you want to know the percentages of men and women in television commercials and you examine a random sample of commercials between 11 A.M. and 4 P.M. for one month.

   a. What is the population?

   b. What is the sample?

   c. Is the sample likely to be representative of the population? Explain.

   d. If you think the sample is not likely to be representative, what ideas do you have about how to arrive at a more representative sample?

5. Suppose you want to know whether members of a professional organization of physicians are satisfied with their work. You find a list of the members of the organization and select names at random from the list to question. Everyone you select answers your questions.

   a. What is the population?

   b. What is the sample?

   c. Is the sample likely to be representative of the population? Explain.

   d. If you think the sample is not likely to be representative, what ideas do you have about how to arrive at a more representative sample?

6. Suppose you want to know how many freshmen at your university watch soap operas and whether men or women watch more soap operas. You divide the freshman class into men and women and then select (at random) the same percentage of men and women to call as occur in the freshman class. Everyone you call answers your questions.

   a. What is the population?

   b. What sample design did you use?

   c. Is the sample likely to be representative of the population? Explain.

   d. If you think the sample is not likely to be representative, what ideas do you have about how to arrive at a more representative sample?

7. Suppose you want to know what students who live in the residence halls think about the residence hall cafeteria and you stand outside the cafeteria after breakfast on a Monday to ask every third student leaving the cafeteria to fill in questionnaires you've prepared. Everyone you ask responds.

   a. What is the population?

   b. What is your sample?

   c. Is the sample likely to be representative of the population? Explain.

   d. If you think the sample is not likely to be representative, what ideas do you have about how to arrive at a more representative sample?

8. Suppose Manuel's friend Kim received a grade from a teacher that Kim thought was unfair. Manuel also read a statistical report that students in general think Kim's teacher is a fair grader. What do you think Manuel will think about whether Kim's teacher is a fair grader? (In your answer, discuss the effects of vivid and pallid data.)

9. Suppose a doctor has several patients with Lyme disease whose symptoms went away after taking a particular drug, and the doctor reads in a journal that another drug is more effective in the treatment of the disease. Which drug do you think the doctor will be more likely to recommend to future patients? (In your answer, discuss the effects of vivid and pallid data.)

10. A poll of *Hispanic* readers found that 64.8% of those responding support affirmative action and 35.1% do not support affirmative action. How many Hispanic people support affirmative action?

11. Suppose a reliable poll taker seeks information about Republican voting preferences by questioning a sample of Republicans. The poll taker finds that 52% plan to vote for Candidate A and that 48% plan to vote for Candidate B. The margin of error is +/–3%.

   a. What is the population?

   b. Is Candidate A ahead among Republicans?

12. Suppose a reliable poll taker seeks information about Democrat voting preferences by questioning a sample of Democrats. The poll taker finds that 54% plan to vote for Proposition Q and that 46% plan to vote against Proposition Q. Assume the margin of error is +/–3%.

   a. What is the population?

   b. Is Proposition Q likely to pass in the election? Explain.

Answers

1. True/False

   a. True
   b. False
   c. False
   d. True
   e. True
   f. False
   g. True
   h. False
   i. True
   j. True
   k. False
   l. False

2. Short Answer

   a. Examples will vary.

   b. Examples will vary.

   c. Observing, interviewing, or collecting information about each member of a group to form a generalization about the group

3. Match

   a. f
   b. m
   c. h
   d. b
   e. e
   f. j
   g. k
   h. g

4. a. Men and women in television commercials

   b. A random sample of commercials between 11 A.M. and 4 P.M.

   c. No. Shows that air during the day are different in type from those shown in the evening.

   d. Sample shows from around the clock

5. a. The members of the professional organization of physicians

   b. The persons selected at random from the list

   c. Yes, assuming it's large enough. Random samples tend to be representative.

   d. I'd check the sample size with a good statistician to make sure it was large enough.

6. a. Freshmen at the university

   b. Stratified random sample

   c. Yes, assuming the samples are large enough. Random samples tend to be representative and stratified samples even more so.

   d. I'd check the sample sizes with a statistician.

7. a. Students who live in the residence halls of your university

   b. The students surveyed coming from the cafeteria

   c. No. It doesn't include students who are so dissatisfied that they don't eat at the residence halls. It also doesn't include students who don't eat breakfast. Also, breakfasts may be better or worse than other meals, and the students' recent bad or good experience could cloud their evaluation of the cafeteria.

   d. You could question a random sample of dorm residents about the food, checking with a statistician to find out how large your sample needs to be.

8. I think that Manuel will be more influenced in his thinking by Kim's vivid report than by the pallid statistical data. He'll probably think that Kim's teacher is not a fair grader. (Note: Kim's teacher may have made a mistake in Kim's case, but one mistake or unfair grade does not make someone an unfair grader.)

9. Doctors are just as likely to be subject to the undue influence of vivid data as the rest of us. I think the doctor will probably recommend the drug he had personal experience with.

10. It's impossible to say from this information. First, there are no doubt Hispanic people who are not readers of *Hispanic* and there are readers of *Hispanic* who are not Hispanic. Second, the sample is not random and there's no margin of error reported, so even if the question asked about the number of Hispanic readers who supported affirmative action, there's not enough information to answer the question.

11. a. Republicans

    b. Not necessarily. Given the margin of error, the percentage of Republicans who will vote for Candidate A could be as low as 49% and the percentage who vote for Candidate B could be as high as 51%.

12. a. The population is Democrats.

    b. Not necessarily. From the figures given, a slim majority of Democrats will vote for it, but persons from other parties may outvote the Democrats.

CHAPTER 10
CAUSAL REASONING

This chapter teaches students awareness of multiple causes and effects, the importance of distinguishing contributing factors from necessary or sufficient conditions, the basic steps of a causal study, societal constraints on causal studies, and ways to evaluate reports of causal studies.

SUMMARY

Learning to understand causal claims and evaluate causal reasoning is important because we frequently make decisions about whether to do one thing or another depending on the consequences (causal effects) of the acts. And we decide whether to praise or blame someone for something depending on whether the person is responsible for (caused) something we approve or disapprove of.

The word "cause" means to produce or bring about. Striking a match causes the match to flame; the striking produces or brings about the flame. Causes also prevent effects. Pouring water on the match causes it not to burst into flames when struck.

We frequently talk as if causes and effects follow each other like links in a chain, each cause having one effect and each effect having one cause. But in fact for anything to happen, a variety of causes typically is required, and causes typically have multiple effects. Whether we call something the cause or the effect depends on our interests and purposes. A "side effect" in one situation becomes "the effect" in another. Because of the multiplicity of causes and effects, the relationship between causes and effects is better illustrated by a web than by a chain.

Not all types of causes play the same role in the causal web. A necessary condition is an event that must take place for another event to occur. By knowing that a necessary condition is not present, we can predict that the event it is necessary for definitely is not present.

A sufficient condition is the combination of events that together bring about the effect. When we have evidence that this combination of events is very likely present, we can infer that the effect will very likely result. A contributing factor is an event that partially causes an effect but is neither necessary nor sufficient by itself for the effect to occur. Claims about contributing factors yield less certain predictions. Recognizing that most individual causes are contributing factors helps us avoid the slippery slope fallacy, the assumption that a particular event inevitably results in a distant effect. When making predictions, we must also be on the lookout for multiple effects, some of which may be negative.

160

We frequently use common knowledge or reliable authority as bases of support for causal claims. However, sometimes we need to do our own causal studies. Causal studies typically have three steps: clarify the goal of the study; develop a list of possible, testable causes (hypotheses); and test the hypotheses. Imagination, play, background knowledge, and research are all useful for generating hypotheses. Some indications of possible causes include an unusual event that preceded the effect, a common event among different preceding activities, and correlated events. A hypothesis must be testable to be tested. Very vague hypotheses are untestable because they cannot be disconfirmed.

People who jump from priority in time to causation commit the *post hoc* fallacy. To avoid the post hoc fallacy, ask the following questions: Did the same presumed cause ever happen without the effect? Did the same effect happen without the presumed cause? Is there another possible explanation of the effect?

People who jump to the conclusion that one thing causes another because the two things are correlated commit the correlation fallacy. To avoid the correlation fallacy, ask the following questions about two correlated events: Is there any evidence that one of the events is more likely to cause the other? Is there any evidence that there is no third event that may cause both of them? Is there any evidence that the correlation is sheer coincidence?

An experiment that controls all the possible causes is called a strictly controlled experiment. Priority in time and correlation are sufficient to establish causation in the context of a strictly controlled experiment.

In randomized experiments, researchers compare groups whose members are selected at random. By randomizing the selection of the groups, researchers spread potential causes evenly among the two groups. The potential cause is then added to one of the groups (experimental group), and the other serves as a control group. Because there is always some difference between groups, even when picked at random, there may well be some chance difference between the groups. Differences greater than statisticians would expect to find created by chance are called "statistically significant" differences.

Researchers must be on the lookout for confounding variables (a possible cause, such as researcher or subject expectation, that is inadvertently introduced to the experimental group). In some studies researchers rule out researcher and subject expectations with a *double blind*, keeping the researcher and subjects from knowing which group is the experimental group and which is the control group. Giving the control group placebos, a look-alike pill with no causal efficacy, helps maintain the blind.

A study has external validity when its results can be generalized outside the experimental context.

In a natural experiment, the researcher studies groups that arise naturally. In a natural experiment, researchers hope to find roughly similar groups so they can avoid the correlation fallacy. They also rule out rival hypotheses that explain the correlation.

Causal studies have a number of societal constraints. From ethical considerations, some studies are halted or not allowed at all. Prejudice and economics also determine the subject and method of causal studies.

When you are evaluating reports of causal studies, keep the following questions in mind: Who conducted the study? Who sponsored the study? What sort of study was done? What are the findings? Are the findings controversial?

COMMON PROBLEMS FOR STUDENTS

Students have difficulty recognizing causal claims, so it's useful to spend some time working with them on this. They also have difficulty recognizing instances when inadequate evidence has been given for a causal claim they believe to be true.

A minor point, but one that might throw you if you're not expecting it, is that a surprising number of students confuse the word "causal" with the word "casual." You might want to note that my use of the word "correlation" is broader than the classical usage. My use includes covariations—comparisons made using variables with binary values.

SAMPLE ANSWERS TO EXERCISES

1. a. No, there are multiple effects of eating chocolate. Even if it does create the effect of falling in love, it also causes allergic reactions in some people. A person who suffers an allergic reaction may not feel good after eating chocolate candy.

   b. The conclusion follows with certainty. Water is a necessary condition for petunias to live.

   c. Assuming the computer does not have an auto-save feature enabled, we can be certain that the last five minutes of typing have been lost. Hitting "save" is a necessary condition to saving the paper.

   d. The stove may have a broken or burned out thermocouple, which contributes to its not working. Although having gas is necessary for the stove to work, if the stove does not work, it is not necessarily out of gas.

e. Although fish emulsion helps the plants bloom, they can reasonably be expected to bloom without it; they just may not bloom as much. Not using fish emulsion is a contributing factor to decreased bloom.

f. It does not necessarily follow that the use of fish emulsion will bring blooms. Perhaps the plants have not been watered, or have not gotten sufficient sunlight. Using fish emulsion is a contributing factor to increased bloom.

2. There are no right answers to these questions, as long as students list only causal hypotheses! In the article I read about the sea otters, scientists mentioned that it was mating season and that sometimes males drown the females in the process. The scientists didn't think over-energetic mating was the primary cause, however, and they hadn't figured out what caused the deaths or whether there were multiple causes.

3. a. Testable. We could ask him how he feels about the professor. We could monitor how John reacts to others in positions of authority who are deserving of respect and see whether he removes his hat for them. We would have to define "disrespectful person" first.

b. Untestable. Perhaps if John stated a desire to remove his hat, yet said he was unable to do so as his arms would not move, this could imply a magic force. But it would not be solid proof as the force could decide to allow John to remove the hat.

c. Testable. The black tar around the edges of his hat and his inability to remove the hat when he tried, followed by his explanation, are proof.

d. Testable. Set up control groups and experimental groups of individuals with similar math abilities and administer a math test to the groups, playing Mozart for one group and not for the other. Review the test scores for support or refutation of the hypothesis.

e. Testable. Start out with two similar groups of students who test roughly the same on critical thinking ability, then have one group take a critical thinking class. At the end of the semester, test both groups of students again and compare their scores.

f. No right answer, based on your individual responses

4. a. The support ("Young women . . . exclusively") states a correlation. Correlation is not sufficient to establish the conclusion, which states that there is a causal relation between the two correlated events. Other possible causes (student-teacher ratio) must be excluded. Correlation is relevant to generating a causal hypothesis.

b. The support here (A study . . .) describes a correlation between secondhand smoke and risk of lung cancer. We aren't told whether other possible causes were controlled for. The correlation is useful for generating a causal hypothesis but does not establish causation. (Because we already know that there's a link between smoking and lung cancer, it makes sense for us to take precautions against secondhand smoke. Staying away from it is not likely to harm us, and doing so may be beneficial.)

c. The support provides post hoc information. First, Sue dials Ginny's beeper. Second, the telephone rings. We have additional background knowledge that people who call after being beeped are usually calling because they were beeped; therefore, it's not unreasonable for us to conclude that Ginny called because she was beeped. However, Ginny's call could be coincidental. This has happened to me. I made up this example after beeping a friend and receiving a coincidental call from him. The post hoc information in the support is relevant to generating a causal hypothesis.

d. Helmut provides post hoc evidence. It's relevant to generating a causal hypothesis but not sufficient for establishing one. Perhaps the popcorn was old and the kernels would not have popped anyway. Helmut needs to do an experiment to rule out this possibility. He could compare how the corn pops when the popper's been warmed up three minutes with how the corn pops when the popper has not been warmed up three minutes.

e. The evidence in this support is post hoc and correlation. Both are relevant to generating a causal hypothesis but are not sufficient to establish one. To establish a causal link, the researchers need to explain how they ruled out other possible causes of the drop in the teen pregnancy rate. (A new wave of abstinence? A new neighborhood free clinic?) Nonetheless, it does seem reasonable to believe that free medical and contraceptive services at school would lower the teen pregnancy rate, assuming that teens are as sexually active as before and that they have no other sources for information and contraception.

5. a. The children in the study are from "white and middle-class neighborhoods" and "recruited from church-affiliated kindergartens in a southern city." How far one can generalize beyond the study depends on whether children from different cultural backgrounds can be expected to behave similarly.

b. This study could be considered as having questionable external validity if one takes into consideration the environment in which the girls are raised. Perhaps another group of girls would react differently based on their upbringing.

6. There is no right answer regarding whether you agree with the author; the causal conclusion has been identified below.

    a. The author is accusing parents "who are horrified that . . ." of the slippery slope fallacy (today a lollipop-stick sword, tomorrow an AK-47). The author points out that children become violent because of other factors (physical and emotional abuse). I expect the author is right that some people exaggerate the effects of playing with toy weapons. Still, I wonder about the role of these toys as part of a culture of violence. It would be interesting to see whether children from cultures less violent than ours were raised surrounded with violent images and toys.

    b. This article questions a study of the relationship between tattoos and HIV infection. The writers suggest that the researchers did not consider alternative explanations of the higher incidence of HIV among tattooed subjects. They also find the study's subjects (drug-dependent outpatients) unrepresentative of the general population, a finding that implies the study has questionable external validity.

       Please note that the author does not quote the researchers as attributing the difference in HIV infection rate to the tattooing.

7. a. Yes. The study of the relationship between abuse and later violent activity can only be done using a natural experiment. It would be wrong for an experimenter to create two random samples of children and abuse one group to learn whether the abused children engage in violence more frequently than the other children. I don't see a moral problem with offering toy weapons to one of two similar groups of children to test the hypothesis that children who use toy weapons tend to become violent in their later years. However, it would be difficult to control for all the other possible variables, and it might be difficult to gather sufficient data without invading the privacy or limiting the autonomy of the subjects.

    b. Loimer and Werner could study the relationship between HIV infection and tattooing that occurs among the general population. Gathering the data would be complicated, but I see no moral concerns, assuming researchers can gather the data without invasions of privacy.

8. There's no right answer to this question.

9. There's more to say about this report than the following questions elicit. First, the report gives information about the fourth study relevant to the question of external validity. The white wine's chemical makeup that may have played a causal role varies from batch to batch of wine.

Also, the report mentions other factors that could explain correlations between drinking wine and health—namely, the better diet and health care of wine drinkers (because they're better educated and more well-to-do) and the fact that wine tends to be consumed with meals.

a. Who conducted the study? "Is Only Red Wine Fine" refers to a number of studies: a Danish study (researchers unnamed), published in the *British Medical Journal*; a study done by unnamed researchers from Harvard Medical School; a study (researchers unnamed) at Kaiser Permanente Medical Center in Oakland; and a study by the Jordan Heart Research Foundation in Montclair, New Jersey, presented at the American Chemical Society Conference in Chicago.

b. Who sponsored the study? No sponsorship for the Danish study is given. I assume that Harvard Medical School, Kaiser Permanente, and Jordan Heart Research Foundation sponsored the other studies, but perhaps not. Maybe they just provided researchers and the wine industry paid the tab.

c. What sort of study was done? The only study that was described in any detail was the Jordan Heart Research study. The design of this study doesn't fit into any of the methodologies described in this chapter. My guess is that the Kaiser study was epidemiological (a natural experiment). I suspect that they gathered information about 81,000 people who were already drinking.

d. What are the findings? The studies all find correlations: wine drinking with lower death rates from cardiovascular disease and stroke (Danish), a drink or two of any alcohol beverage and risk of heart attack lowered by one-half (Harvard), white wine and lowest risk of coronary artery disease (Kaiser), 6 ounces of wine per day and a drop in free radicals in the blood as well as a decrease in the blood's ability to clot (Jordan).

e. Are other studies reported that agree or disagree with the findings of the featured studies? There appears to be a conflict between the Danish study and the Harvard study if deaths from cardiovascular disease include heart attacks. The Danish study found that nonwine alcoholic drinks are not correlated with lower death rates from cardiovascular disease. The Harvard study found a correlation between any alcoholic beverage and lowered risk of heart attack.

10. The issue of sufficient evidence in support of a claim is a relative issue. The answers below outline the claim; the issue of sufficient support is subjective, yet considerations are listed.

a. The ad implies that AT&T technology increases respect for parents and emotional closeness with distant family members. If this were true, it would serve as a reason for families to use AT&T. The information in the ad, however, isn't directly relevant to the conclusion that AT&T hopes the reader will draw. For example, "daughters can have an easier time listening" is ambiguous. Is the daughter's listening easier because there's less static on the line or because she appreciates what her mother says? There's also a weasel word—"can"—in the claim. A similar kind of weaseling occurs with "barriers between loved ones." AT&T doesn't explicitly claim to help break emotional barriers, which is what the audience hopes for. Instead, it says that "family members are finding it easy to comprehend even the subtlest inflections of a familiar voice." But understanding subtle inflections doesn't guarantee emotional closeness. The inflection could express some form of put-down.

b. The ad claims that Depo-Provera is more than 99% effective as birth control. It also notes some of the most common "side effects": irregular menstrual bleeding, cessation of menstruation, and weight gain. The advertiser hopes the birth control seeking reader will decide to purchase Depo-Provera. The claims made are relevant to that decision. They are not sufficient, however. The reader needs additional information about the likelihood of suffering from the listed side effects as well as information about other, less common side effects and other birth control methods. The ad does recommend that the reader discuss the risks and benefits of birth control methods with a doctor or other health care provider.

SAMPLE ANSWERS TO READINGS FOR ANALYSIS

David C. Anderson, "The Television Time Bomb: Violence on the Take, a Public Health Issue"

1. We know that the researcher is a psychiatrist in Seattle. Beyond that, we have no information regarding his reliability.

2. A natural study was done using existing documentation regarding the changes in homicide rates and the influx of television into various societies. There was concern regarding the effect of the civil rights movement and the Vietnam war on the numbers, so similar studies were done using Canadian figures.

3. According to the report, "Dr. Centerwall concludes that long-term childhood exposure to television is a causal factor behind half of the homicides committed in

the United States, or about 10,000 homicides annually." The report says the homicide rate among white Americans "nearly doubled." We aren't told what it doubled from. We also aren't given the specific figures of the "biggest surge" that is reported to have occurred after 1965.

4. No studies agreeing or disagreeing were mentioned; however, the author does state that once "corroborated by other researchers, [this study] suggests good reason to worry."

5. The study is relevant to the causal hypothesis that there is some relationship between the introduction of television and the increase in homicides. I don't think there's enough evidence from the study to support a particular causal hypothesis. Among other things, I wonder whether persons who murder watch any more television than those who don't. I also wonder whether the problem was that the children watched TV, or that their *parents* watched TV. Maybe children feel abandoned by parents who are glued to the tube. Also, is the problem TV watching per se or TV watching during the time that parents would otherwise be engaged in activities with their children? Maybe if children watched TV at school and came home to have long conversations with their parents, they wouldn't grow up to murder. On the other hand, given how abusive some parents are, maybe their children are better off watching TV than engaging with them.

    The report notes that Dr. Centerwall considered the effects of age distribution, urbanization, economic conditions, alcohol consumption, capital punishment, civil unrest, and the availability of firearms. I'd like to know more about how he ruled out these and combinations of these as potential explanations of the increased murder rates.

6. Dr. Centerwall suggests educating pediatricians and parents, rating TV shows for violence and requiring that all new TV sets be equipped with time-channel locks that would let parents block violent shows. The article also recommends more day care and after-school programs that would allow working parents to make less use of TV as a baby sitter.

7. No right answer

Marie Winn, "Does Television Itself Nurture Violence?"

1. That perhaps it is a lack of play and parental disciplinary interaction, not violent programming, that have created a more violent society. Winn claims that the study shows a link between TV and murder, not between violent TV shows and murder.

2. By citing research performed by Harry Harlow et al, she also notes that before the TV age, parents disciplined their children; now they plug them into TV.

3. No right answer

4. The information is not sufficient to establish causation. But this author isn't trying to establish causality; she's suggesting possible causes.

5. Assuming her explanation is correct, she says that the remedy requires "reducing or possibly eliminating television itself from the lives of our children." I, too, am concerned about using TV as a baby-sitter for children, but I wonder what alternatives many working parents have. Also, too many parents don't know how to teach their children. I'd like to see community services that help parents raise their children. Children need places to go and things to do that engage them and enable them to see themselves as useful contributors to society. Merely turning off the tube isn't enough to lead children to discover how to become responsible and caring citizens.

6. No right answer

Todd Gitlin, "Imagebusters: The Hollow Crusade against TV Violence"

1. The availability of firearms, the lack of available jobs, and absence of "legitimate parental authority"

2. Gitlin quotes from the American Psychological Association's report *Violence and Youth*: "Many social science disciplines . . . have firmly established that poverty and its contextual life circumstances are major determinants of violence" and "There is considerable evidence that the alarming rise in youth homicides is related to the availability of firearms." He doesn't offer support for the relationship between violence and parental authority, though he mentions that it's a conservative argument he accepts.

3. I'd like to know more about the expertise of the people who prepared the report mentioned.

4. He implies that we should be focusing more attention on reducing poverty and the availability of firearms than we focus on reducing TV violence. Decreasing poverty is worthwhile, even it if doesn't diminish violence. I also see no significant negative effects of making firearms less available to youth.

5. No right answer

Suzanne Braun Levine, "Caution: Children Watching"

1. Dr. Prothrow-Stith doesn't explicitly say, but she implies that education and working with the media are the right approach.

2. Via the analogy with smoking

3. The only information given about her is that she's of the Harvard School of Public Health.

4. I do not understand clearly what precisely she's recommending. However, I question whether the smoking analogy works. I suspect that people are willing to give up or not start smoking because there's strong evidence of a causal connection between smoking and various types of poor health. Unless researchers are able to come up with equally telling evidence of a broad range of negative effects from TV watching (or violent program watching) for an equal percentage of the viewing population, I don't think education will have the same effect.

5. I think it's a great idea. It gives children practice coming up with nonviolent solutions to problems. It won't, however, be of use to those children who have less attentive parents.

6. This question presupposes that there are problems of television violence. The evidence in the above articles does not convince me of the nature of the connection, if there is one. However, I also doubt that any good comes from watching violence, so my personal policy is to avoid it. I choose not to go to violent movies, and I don't watch TV at all (unless I have the flu and am practically brain dead already).

   I also think that many of the ideas suggested in these readings are good ones. The world would be a better place if children and their parents talked about problem solving, if fewer people lived in poverty, and if weapons were less accessible to youth. Moreover, if we refused to watch programs of questionable value, there would be more time for walking under the stars, writing to a maiden aunt, or helping a neighbor child with her homework. The possibilities are endless.

7. No right answer

COMMENTS ON WRITING IDEAS

The first idea and the last idea would make good freewrites for class discussion. The second and third ideas give students an opportunity to practice evaluating causal reasoning. The third one also reinforces the idea that good writing includes rethinking. The fourth idea gives students practice critiquing reports of causal studies.

CLASSROOM ACTIVITIES

Solutions to the Problem of Violence

Description: After reading the above readings for analysis, volunteers from the class role-play a panel of "experts" who offer descriptions of and solutions to the problem of violence in American society. The rest of the class questions the experts about whether their causal claims are stated clearly enough to test and whether they've provided ample evidence to rule out alternative possible causes. The class then discusses the problem of making decisions without scientific certainty and proposes policies for responding to the problem of violence in American society.

Purpose: To develop the ability to distinguish adequate from inadequate support for a causal claim

To improve speaking and listening skills

To develop the capacity to think for oneself

To develop problem-solving ability

Designing Causal Studies

Description: Students select a causal problem for study. As a class, they generate hypotheses to test. They then divide into groups. One of the groups is a grant-funding agency. The other groups are researchers. Each group of researchers selects a hypothesis to test and decides the best way to test the hypothesis. The researchers present their study proposals to the funding agency group, and the funding agency decides which study to fund.

Purpose: To develop the ability to think creatively

To improve understanding of how to test causal hypotheses

To develop the ability to work productively with others

Courting Confusion about Causality

Description: Students do guided freewrites beginning "When it comes to causality I am confused about . . . " Before they begin, tell them that they will win treats for their confusions. Then let them write for about 10 minutes. When they have finished have a short class discussion about the categories for prizes, such as "longest list," "deepest confusion," and so on. Then ask the students to read their confusions in small groups and have each group recommend freewrites for the treats. Bring enough treats for everyone.

Purpose: To develop the ability to think creatively

To improve self-awareness of ignorance and confusion

To improve self-confidence

To achieve a deeper understanding of the complexity of causal thinking

QUIZ ITEMS AND ANSWERS

1. True/False

    a. _____   A cause can bring something about or prevent something from happening.

    b. _____   For each cause there's one primary effect.

    c. _____   A web metaphor works better to illustrate the relations among causes and effects than a chain metaphor.

    d. _____   Whether an effect of a drug is called a "side effect" depends on whether the effect is the selling feature of the drug.

    e. _____   In the following, a bulb is asserted to be a necessary condition for turning on a lamp: "If there's no bulb in the lamp, you can't turn the lamp on."

f. _____ If a contributing factor of an event doesn't happen, then you may infer that the event will not happen.

g. _____ If smoking were a sufficient condition of lung cancer, then everyone who smoked would develop lung cancer.

h. _____ According to James L. Adams, the attitude that "playfulness is for children only" blocks creativity.

i. _____ When you are trying to come up with causal hypotheses, correlations are irrelevant.

j. _____ Establishing correlation alone is insufficient for establishing causality.

k. _____ In a causal study, a variable is a possible cause of an effect.

l. _____ Selecting members of control and experimental groups at random increases the likelihood that the groups will be similar.

2. Short Answer

   a. What are three questions to ask to avoid the *post hoc* fallacy?

   b. What are three questions to ask to avoid the correlation fallacy?

   c. What is a confounding variable?

   d. When does a study have external validity?

3. Are any of the following causal hypotheses untestable or questionably testable as they are presently stated? Explain.

   a. Lazy teachers contribute to low student morale.

   b. A grade point average of B or better contributes to a student's obtaining a job paying $20,000 a year within one year of graduation.

   c. Carol's computer won't turn on because of a contrary poltergeist.

4. Earl wanted to see if the nutritional pill he'd ordered really worked, so he took one with his breakfast; within an hour he had plenty of energy for the day. He decided that the pill gave him the energy.

   a. What is Earl's conclusion?

   b. Has Earl committed the post hoc or correlation fallacy? Explain.

5. Katrina noticed that people in Japan weigh less on average than people in the United States, and she also noted that people in Japan eat more rice than people in the United States, so Katrina decided to add rice to her diet to lose weight.

   a. What is Katrina's conclusion?

   b. Does Katrina have sufficient evidence for it? Explain.

6. Read this passage and answer the questions that follow.

Long Beach—When it came to school uniforms, Principal Shawn Ashley was once a serious doubter. Now he wears one . . .

For those who still question the value of uniforms in schools, Ashley has one answer: Look at the numbers, look at the reduction of crime at the city's public schools.

The number of school fights is down by half. Suspensions are down by one-third. Every measurable criminal activity is down in public schools throughout the city, from the richest neighborhoods to the poorest [now that uniforms are mandatory for elementary and middle school students].[1]

   a. What causal claim is implied in this passage about the relationship between students wearing school uniforms and crime in the schools? (Does it state a necessary condition, a sufficient condition, or a contributing factor?)

   b. What evidence is provided for the implied causal claim in this passage?

   c. Is the evidence sufficient to establish the implied causal conclusion?

Answers

1. True/False

   a. True
   b. False
   c. True
   d. True
   e. True
   f. False
   g. True
   h. True
   i. False
   j. True
   k. True
   l. True

---

[1] J. Michael Kennedy, "Student Grades Up, Crime Down with Uniforms." Copyright © 1995 Los Angeles Times. Reprinted by permission.

2. Short Answer

   a. Did the same presumed cause ever happen without the effect?

      Did the same effect ever happen without the presumed cause?

      Is there another possible explanation of the effect?

   b. Is there evidence that one of the events is more likely to cause the other?

      Is there evidence that there is no third event that may cause the correlated events?

      Is there evidence that there is no causal explanation of the correlation?

   c. A possible cause introduced to the experimental group other than the possible cause being tested

   d. When the setting of the study is similar to future settings or when you can generalize from the study to other settings

3. a. "Lazy" and "morale" are vague. They need to be precisely defined before this claim can be tested.

   b. This claim is precisely stated. It's testable.

   c. Because of the alleged poltergeist's contrary behavior, there's no way of testing this statement.

4. a. Earl's conclusion is that the pill gave him the energy.

   b. Yes, Earl committed the post hoc fallacy. He concluded that the pill gave him the energy because his energy level went up after taking the pill.

5. a. Katrina's conclusion is that rice contributes to lower body weight.

   b. No, she doesn't have sufficient evidence. There are other possible differences between Japanese and Americans (including average height) that could account for the difference in average weight.

6. a. That wearing school uniforms contributes to a reduction in crime. If the uniforms had been sufficient for crime prevention, there would be no crime afterward. If it had been necessary for crime prevention, then there would have been crime everywhere in the school before the uniforms were introduced.

   b. With the introduction of uniforms for elementary and middle schools, measurable criminal activity in public schools is down throughout the city. Not specifically mentioned but implied is that introduction of the uniforms came before the reduction in crime.

c. To answer this question, let's look at the questions to ask to avoid the correlation fallacy.

Is there evidence that one of the events is more likely to cause the other? Yes, it's more likely that wearing the uniforms contributed to the decrease in crime because wearing the uniforms came first and also because of background knowledge we have about why students started wearing the uniforms.

Is there evidence that there is no third event that may have caused the correlated events? What could this third event be? Perhaps stricter administrations in the schools, which led to dress codes and to different penalties for infractions. No evidence is provided in this passage to rule this out.

I'm inclined to think that the school uniforms had something to do with the decrease in crime. I can think of reasons why this might be so (no gang-related clothing, fewer "odd" clothes that trigger taunting, fewer temptations to steal). Nonetheless, the evidence would have been stronger if schools with similar types of administrations from similar neighborhoods had been divided into control and experimental groups, with the control groups continuing as before and the experimental groups wearing uniforms.

APPENDIX
GROUP PROJECT

STEP 1 (Due: *)* Each person in the group shall provide one article or written transcript of an interview with an expert on the group's topic, with copies for every group member and for the instructor.

STEP 2 (Due: *)* Everyone shall have read the articles and *written* a list of the main points of agreement and disagreement among the articles. Students will have time in class to discuss their findings with each other and make decisions about additional research they need to do.

STEP 3 (Due: *)* Pro and Con papers
Each group is responsible for producing (at least) two 5-page argumentative papers, each one from a different point of view, on your group's topic.

In each paper, students should do the following:

A. Write an Argument

1. Describe a problem and recommend a solution.

2. Provide at least three main supports for the recommended solution.

3. Provide subsupport for at least two of the main supports.

4. Raise and respond to at least one counterconsideration.

5. Define at least one key term.

6. Have an effective introduction and conclusion.

7. Be based on information from at least three sources, with each quotation or summary footnoted. Include full bibliographical data. If you are quoting an article, for example, give the name of the author, the title of the article, the title of the newspaper, book, magazine in which the article was published, the date of publication, and page numbers. For books, also give the city and publisher.

B. Write an Evaluation of Your Argument

1. Discuss the acceptability of your argument's support.

Based on personal experience or expertise: For each quotation or summary, explain whether the person quoted or summarized is a witness or expert on the point quoted or summarized and discuss how reliable that witness or expert is by answering the relevant questions in Chapter 7 of the textbook. If you are making claims on the basis of your own personal experience or expertise, answer these questions for your own claims.

Based on inference: Discuss the acceptability, relevance, and sufficiency of the subsupport. Pay particular attention to any subconclusions based on an argument from analogy, an argument from a sample to a population, or an argument with a causal conclusion.

2. Discuss the relevance of your argument's support. Have you strawpersoned the other side in your statement of counterconsiderations? Is your support relevant to the needs, values, and goals of the persons you hope to convince? Do you have any false background beliefs that undermine the relevance of your support?

3. Discuss the sufficiency of your support. Is your conclusion stated more strongly than is justified by your support? Have you considered and responded to all relevant counterconsiderations? Have you included all the relevant evidence and values in favor of your conclusion? Would a skeptical audience find your support sufficient?

STEP 4 (Due:) Group presentation

Evaluation Checklist for Group Presentations

Content:

A. Did you illustrate the primary stages of deciding how to act?

* * Did you define a problem from a number of points of view and argue for a definition of the problem you found most convincing? (Review Chapter 2 for additional information about defining a problem.)

* * Did you describe a number of different solutions for the problem as you defined it? Did you identify and weigh the pros and cons of these solutions? (Review Chapter 2 for additional information about coming up with solutions and identifying and weighing their pros and cons.)

* * Did you argue for a solution to the problem you defined and describe the action you personally will take toward putting that solution into effect?

B. Did you show the depth of your thought during your decision making?

* * Did you define key terms related to your problem and its solution?

* * Did you identify and compensate for slanting in the alternative descriptions of your problem and in descriptions of the pros and cons of proposed solutions?

* * Did you question the acceptability of key supports made by you and those you disagree with?

* * Did you question the strength of inferences in any of the following types of arguments made by you and others?

    * * argument from analogy

    * * causal reasoning

    * * generalizing from a sample

* * Did you willingly admit your areas of confusion and ignorance?

Format

A. Did you form a panel, do a skit, stage a debate, sing a song, dance, produce a video, or use any other creative format to present your material? Some formats that have worked well in the past include these:

A panel of students role-played experts and interested laypersons giving pros and cons about legalizing marijuana for medicinal purposes. A moderator introduced and questioned the panel. After the panel made short presentations and questioned each other, the students stopped role-playing and began to evaluate the information and arguments in their own presentations.

A panel of students discussed the topic of California's "three strikes" law. One student introduced the pro side, a second student developed the support, and a third student critiqued the information and argument on the pro side. The same format was used for the con side. Afterward, another student summarized the conclusion the group as a whole reached after sorting through the issues.

A group of students wrote and performed a play on the subject of euthanasia. Roles included a young man dying of AIDS, family members, a lover, a doctor, a nurse, a medical ethics specialist, a clergy member.

B. Did you use some sort of visual or tactile aid in your presentation?

FORMS

Student Self-Evaluation Forms:

Group Paper Participation

Group Topic:

Your Name:

Number of articles contributed _____

First draft: nothing, a few points, a developed outline, a complete draft

Synthesizing ideas from drafts: nothing or very little/average/did most of the work

Evaluating the draft's support: nothing or very little/average/did most of the work

Rewriting of drafts: nothing or very little/average/did most of the work

Typing of final draft: nothing or very little/average/did most of the work

Other comments/explanations:

What overall grade would you give yourself for your involvement in the group paper?
_____

What grade would you give others in your group? List name and grade.

	Name	**Grade**
1.	_____	_____
2.	_____	_____
3.	_____	_____
4.	_____	_____
5.	_____	_____
6.	_____	_____
7.	_____	_____

Comments:

Group Presentation Participation

Group Topic:

Your name:

Number of articles beyond the paper research:

Contributing ideas for the format: none/few/average/lots

Developing the visual aid: none/a little/average/lots

How many class meetings did you miss?

Time you spent at group meetings outside of class: Typically left early or didn't go, average attendance, attended every meeting and stayed the whole time.

Other comments/explanations:

What overall grade would you give yourself for your involvement in the group presentation? _____

What grade would you give others in your group for their involvement? List name and grade.

Name   **Grade**

1. _____   _____

2. _____   _____

3. _____   _____

4. _____   _____

5. _____   _____

6. _____   _____

7. _____   _____

8. _____   _____

Comments:

Student Evaluation Form for Group Presentations

Name of Group:

1. How would you rate the group's illustration of the primary stages of deciding how to act?

    ___ Excellent ____ Very Good ____ OK ____ Poor ____ Very Poor

    Comments:

2. How would you rate the group's engaging in questioning and evaluating their own thinking and the thinking of others?

    ___ Excellent ____ Very Good ____ OK ____ Poor ____ Very Poor

    Comments:

3. How effective was the group's format and visual aid?

    ___ Excellent ____ Very Good ____ OK ____ Poor ____ Very Poor

    Comments:

4. Do you have any other comments about individual group members or the group as a whole?